One God | many gods

God | gods

Bible Studies
for Postmodern Times

CONCORDIA PUBLISHING HOUSE · SAINT LOUIS

Authors

Tom Couser, Mark Eiken, Joan Lilley, Kurt Mews, William Moorhead, Beth Ortstadt, Sara Pfeiffer, Dave Rahberg, Jay Reed, Nikki Rochester, and Matt Schaefer

Editor

Tom Nummela

Your comments and suggestions concerning the material are appreciated. Please write the Product Manager, Youth Bible Studies, Concordia Publishing House, 3558 S. Jefferson Avenue, St. Louis, MO 63118-3968.

6   7   8   9   10   07   06   05   04

Contents

Introduction

About <u>One God, Many Gods</u>

Our postmodern times are marked by multiculturalism and extreme toleration. Christians no longer need travel halfway around the world to encounter other faiths—people of those faiths are living next door, building houses of worship in our neighborhoods, and finding converts among our friends. The people of our world have many gods, each of them worshiped in particular ways. This growing multiculturalism is coupled with the notion in postmodern thought that all beliefs should be tolerated except intolerance of another person's beliefs. (A more complete examination of postmodern thinking is provided later in this introduction. It is adapted from the introduction to *Solid Truth,* CPH 1998, stock number 20-2426.)

One God, Many Gods is a Bible study resource for these times. Christianity and 11 other religious faiths are examined and compared with a goal of identifying the central teachings of each and provide some tools for Christians who encounter people of other faiths in their daily lives. The subjects and the Bible studies in this book are appropriate for both high school young people and adults. For those who might have opportunity to combine youth and adults in an intergenerational setting, some suggestions are provided later in this introduction.

Each of the 12 studies follows a similiar format: the focus, objectives, and a simple outline of the lesson are found at the beginning of the study, followed by three additional pages describing the study in detail. Each study includes two photocopiable pages, an overview of the religion in that study and a Bible study page. (The Christianity study has a slightly longer overview and an additional resource page.)

A handy *comparison chart* is found at the back of the book. All 12 religions are summarized side-by-side on sheets that can be copied (preferably on six 11″ × 17″ pages) and posted side by side. Post this chart in the classroom where you teach. Encourage participants to note the similarities and differences among the religions in the six areas compared. The material for this chart is drawn from the overviews found in each study.

Why Study Other Religions?

Religion seems to be inherent in all cultures and all people. It has been said that there are no true atheists. Everyone believes in a god; we need only ask "Which one?" The study of religion then is a study of people and their core beliefs. Those who undertake such study may benefit in many ways:

- **We may better understand people of other faiths,** and not fear or avoid them but be able to interact with them from a base of knowledge. We will have "points of contact" from which may come conversations.

- **We may be able to demonstrate our sincere love for them as people** and learn how to help them without offending them.

- **We may grow in compassion for the 3.7 billion people who do not know the one, true God.** They are people who need the Gospel, who do not know the benefit of God's grace in His Word and sacraments.

- **We may be better able to avoid their false religious views and hold more firmly to our Christian faith.** It can be helpful to "test the metal" of our convictions against the beliefs of others.

- **We are not alone.** Arnold Toynbee said it this way, "The impact of Western culture upon Eastern societies will soon be followed by an equally profound influence of Eastern cultures upon the West." We cannot avoid increased contact with other religions in the twenty-first century, but we can be prepared for such contact.

- **We have a compelling need to share Jesus Christ and the grace we have received with others.** To a world with many gods, we can offer the blessing of faith in the one God who is the only Creator, Redeemer, and Sanctifier of all people. This is a truth that we cannot help but share.

Suggestions for Adapting and Using These Studies

It is not required that all 12 studies in this book be taught nor that they be taught in a particular order. While most groups will benefit from reviewing the basic teachings of Christianity in session 1, some may prefer to skip this study or use it as a conclusion. (You may desire even more background study in the Christian faith before or after tackling these studies. *Solid Truth: Bible Studies for Postmodern Teens* is a set of 12 topical studies based on the Apostles' Creed. It would be logical choice for youth Bible classes.)

If you decide to use only some of the studies initially, consider these points as you make your choices:

- **What religions are prominent in current events right now?** As this book was being developed tensions were high in the Mideast (where Islam is the predominant religion) and the Winter Olympics were being held in Japan (where most people practice a combination of Shinto and Buddhism). That would suggest that in four weeks, a class might tackle sessions 1, 4, 5, and 6.

- **What religions are prominent in your community?** It is natural for young people and adults alike to be curious about the beliefs of their neighbors. In addition, these studies can strengthen their ability to engage in faith conversations with those of other faiths.

- **What religions are prominent in the media?** During 1997, some movies that were popular included *Seven Years in Tibet,* which featured Buddhism, and *Phenomenon,* starring John Travolta, a recent convert to Scientology. Entertainers, sports figures, and other leaders often are held up as ideals. It makes sense that we know about their religions they promote.

Finally, while these studies as outlined will meet the needs for many groups, do not hesitate to invest time and energy in making them fit the needs and characteristics of your group more fully. Adapt activities that don't quite suit you. Add questions or discussions that will help your group learn more effectively. Such adaptation is appropriate, perhaps even necessary, for the best possible results.

Resources

It may be helpful to have some additional resources available for "on the spot" research during these studies. Several of the studies include lists of such books. Among them are:

Churches in America, Thomas Manteufel, CPH, 1994

How to Respond series, CPH, 1995, including

Judaism, Erwin J Kolb

Muslims, Ernest Hahn

Satanism, Bruce G. Frederickson

The Latter-day Saints, Edgar P. Kaiser

Jehovah's Witnesses, Herbert Kern

The Cults, Hubert R. Beck

The New Age Movement, Philip H. Lochhaas

Dictionary of Cults, Sects, Religions, and the Occult, George A. Mather and Larry A. Nichols, Zondervan, 1993

Handbook of Today's Religions, Josh McDowell and Don Stewart, Campus Crusade for Christ, 1983

Abingdon Dictionary of Living Religions, Keith Crim, general editor, Abingdon, 1981

A particularly handy resource might be the phone book and "yellow pages" from your community. They provide tangible evidence of the presence of these other faiths among you.

Internet resources abound on religions of all kinds. Anyone with internet access can easily locate many sources of information. Several internet sites on the worldwide web are mentioned in these studies. As with all such sites, the addresses are subject to change without notice. Use your favorite "web brouser" or search engine. Be aware that, while information is plentiful on the web, critical evaluation is not. It is frequently necessary to verify the accuracy of information in a number of sources. Exercise spiritual discernment as you browse, "test the spirits" against the truth of God's Word, and seek the theological judgment of your pastor or other knowledgeable people whenever you question the soundness of the information you find.

Postmodern Thought

We live in an age of diversity. Our once rather monolithic culture is rapidly becoming a stew of nationalities and cultures. Each ingredient retains its particular flavor and texture even as it is mingled with many others. The result is no longer the melting pot some envisioned, but a multicultural challenge of significant proportions.

What is more alarming, however, is that there is an even greater cultural challenge facing us—a cultural shift such as may not have been seen since the Enlightenment and the beginning of the so-called modern era. Many scholars suggest that we are seeing the end of modernity and the beginning of the postmodern era, a shift in world view that will affect all corners of our society—including, and perhaps most significantly, the church.

In postmodernity we are witnessing the end of humanity's dream that reason, human intelligence, and scientific advancement would bring about dramatic, lasting solutions to society's problems. A new social mindset is at work in the children and grandchildren of the Baby Boom generation.

Postmodern thought will bring many challenges to the church's ministry over the next 20 years—initially with teenagers and young adults, but increasingly in all areas of the church's work. It is self-evident that at some point in the future, the church will be populated by people living in, and culturally attuned to, the postmodern age.

In the modern era, boundaries were strong. People had a sense of place and of what was expected of them in that place. Loyalties were strong, and people identified themselves by membership in community, vocation, and family. With boundaries strong, the need for individual vision was not great. In the postmodern age, we are seeing the falling away of boundaries of all kinds—family structure, political and geographic isolation, moral expectations, and denominational loyalty. The need for this age will be a strong vision—a personally held understanding of the purpose and value of each association and activity. It may be that the church has a chance at providing just such a vision. This book is one step in that direction.

Using This Study with Intergenerational Groups

Adults and youth—even parents and their teenagers—can study the Bible together. While that truth should come as no surprise, such study opportunities are rare in most congregations. Recent statistics have shown the power of faith conversations among parents and teens to enhance the spiritual development of teens. Also clear is the need for congregations to assist and support the family in the task of nurturing faith in children and young people (see *Congregations at Crossroads,* © 1995 by Search Institute, pages 21–22).

If you are willing to provide a faith-enhancing opportunity for intergenerational Bible study using this book, keep the following points in mind.

- **Let the voices of youth and adults be heard equally.** Let youth share in oral reading, small group leadership tasks, and responses to questions as frequently as adults. The young people may initially be somewhat shy. You may occasionally have to encourage or prompt them into greater participation. Adults are often accustomed to group process. You may occasionally have to restrain them by directing questions or appointing roles without waiting for volunteers.

- **Be sensitive to the self-consciousness of some young people.** Especially if intergenerational experiences are new to your congregation, some young people may be intimidated in groups of adults. Use the warm-up activities, such as questions that require verbal responses from every person, to "level the playing field" for youth participation.

- **Remember that many adults, as well as young people, are reluctant to read aloud.** Choose volunteers for such tasks based on your advance knowledge of reading ability or the genuine eagerness of a volunteer to read.

- **Use a variety of group experiences to facilitate interaction.** Build group relationships by moving from activities requiring low level of self-revelation toward those with greater degrees of intimacy. When creating small groups for discussion and personal sharing, you might start with activities that group adults together and youth together. Mixed groups of four-to-six, with at least two youth in each group, could follow. A "next step" might be preliminary discussion in pairs of adults and pairs of youth. Then bring pairs together in groups of four (two adults and two youth, preferably not related) for further discussion. For more intimate sharing, pair parents with their teenagers and other adults with nonrelated teens.

Christianity
A Standard for Comparison

Colossians 2:6–12

Study Outline: Christianity

Activity	Time Suggested	Materials Needed
Opening Activities		
Introduction	8 minutes	Index cards, masking tape
Prayer	2 minutes	(optional: a treat or prize)
Studying the Word		
The Christian Faith	10 minutes	Bibles; copies of Resource Page 1A (2 pages)
The Heart of the Gospel	20 minutes	Bibles; copies of Resource Page 1B
Applying the Word (Choose one)		
How Would You Respond?	10 minutes	One copy of Resource Page 1C
Contemporary Encounters	10 minutes	
Closing Prayer	5 minutes	

Opening Activities

Introduction

Before class write each of the following words or phrases on a separate index card. If possible, have one card for each anticipated participant (the words and phrases are taken from Resource Pages 1A–1B:): *Adam and Eve; Abraham; Augustine; Baptism; disciples; eternal life; Gospel; grace; Holy Communion; Law; Paul;* and *sin.*

Divide the participants into two teams. Then challenge the class to a quiz of Christian vocabulary. Each person in turn will draw one card from those you have prepared. That person's team will get three points if the person can fully describe the term in 15 seconds without help, one point for a partial description or if he or she receives help from a team member, and no points for a wrong definition or no definition. You will be the judge of correct answers and will time each person.

Play the game for 7-10 minutes and announce the winning team. (You may wish to reward them in some way.) Then say, "The people we come into contact with each week may come from different religions or have no religion at all. For many of them the names and the phrases from our quiz—words that many of you found so easy to explain—are new concepts without meaning for these people." Invite a volunteer to read the objectives for this study aloud, pointing out that, as the class begins a course of study about other religions, an important starting point is a solid understanding of the Christian faith.

Opening Prayer

Then lead the class in prayer using words of your own or the following: "Gracious Creator, help us grow in our knowledge of You and our willingness to tell others about the life-changing power You have brought into our lives. We have friends, acquaintances, and co-workers who do not know the price Jesus paid to redeem all of us. Through Your Holy Spirit, give us the words and the opportunities to reflect Your grace to them. In Jesus' name we pray. Amen."

Studying the Word

The Christian Faith

Distribute copies of both pages of Resource Page 1A. Read aloud, or have volunteers read aloud, each of the sections. Discuss any questions the participants have. You may wish to have some Bible reference books or a Christian encyclopedia available for research. Or assign the questions no one can answer to interested individuals for research during the week.

Then discuss the following questions:

1. What do you think has created so many Christian denominations? What are the good and bad results of such variety? (Denominational differences can result from differing opinions on matters of organization, governance, and ritual, as well as varying interpretations of some doctrines. On the one hand, lack of structural unity may cause some offense; on the other, it provides many options in a world that is used to having choices.)

2. What other names would you have added to the section on "Significant People"? Why do you think they were important? (Answers will vary according to the participants' experience and background.)

3. Why are the church's teachings about Jesus *Christ* central to the *Christ*ian faith? (Accept all answers for now; this topic will be fully explored on Resource Page 1B, "The Heart of the Gospel.")

The Heart of the Gospel

Distribute copies of Resource Page 1B, "The Heart of the Gospel." Invite the participants to read the Bible passage (as printed on the page or out of their Bibles) and think about and respond to the questions. The questions are not easy ones; they will require serious thought. When the class has had some time for this work, discuss the questions incorporating the following comments:

1. "Received"—our faith in Christ is God's gift, not our action; "live in Him"—the new life in Christ is also the result of the Spirit at work in us; "rooted and built up"—Christ is the foundation (root) and the framework for our faith and life; "strengthened in the faith"— He provides the strength we require to resist temptation and remain close to Him; "overflowing with thankfulness"—what else can we do for all that than give thanks?

2. The participants' examples will vary according to their experiences. Help them see that *all* tradition is not hollow, but that which no longer has significance in our faith life. Examples might include going to church out of habit or coercion or seeking personal gain at the expense of others. (More specifics will be described in other studies in this book as we explore other religions.)

3. Many responses are possible. Christ's love for us, His perfect obedience, His intimate knowledge of our needs, and His resurrection-power are examples.

4. Paul points specifically to the "death of sin" in our lives through Baptism and the ongoing work of the Holy Spirit and the resurrection to new life. Allow volunteers to talk about the importance of these things in their lives.

Applying the Word (Choose one)

How Would You Respond?

Use this activity or the one that follows, but not both, unless you have extra time.

Make a copy of Resource Page 1C. Divide the class into three groups, separate the three case studies on the page, and give one to each group. (If your class is small, simply discuss the case studies one at a time with the entire class.) Direct the participants to read and discuss the case studies and formulate a response based on what they have learned in this session. After about five minutes, discuss each case study briefly. Make sure the following points are included.

1. Redirect the participants to the Central Teaching and Other Major Teachings sections of Resource Page 1A. Point out that Christian denominations in fact have many points of agreement.

2. Again use the resource page to indicate the important questions in this matter: What does this church believe and teach about Jesus Christ? Do they acknowledge the triune God, original sin, and God's grace as our only cure for sin? Do they teach the Bible's doctrines of Law and Gospel accurately?

3. Be sensitive to the fact that people in the class may *live* this situation. While different churches are not the ideal for some practical reasons—Sunday morning schedules and eventual raising of children among them—affirm that what is of chief importance is the centrality of Jesus Christ and salvation through Him.

Contemporary Encounters

Use this activity or the previous one, but not both, unless you have extra time.

Write these three phrases on newsprint or on the board: (a) *Speak love*, (b) *Share the Gospel*, and (c) *Stay alert*. Briefly discuss these three principles to keep in mind as we talk about our faith with others: (a) always speak with love in your words and hearts (1 Peter 3:15–17); (b) always share the Gospel and its impact in your own life (Romans

If your class is large and you expect to create more than three groups, prepare one copy of Resource Page 1C for every three groups you will have. Give the same situation to two or more groups. When the groups report, invite one group to volunteer their response, then allow the others group(s) to affirm or expand on the first group's suggestions.

1:16–17); and (c) be on guard so that you are not led astray by the false beliefs of others (1 John 2:24).

Give some volunteers the opportunity to practice using these guidelines in conversation with each other. Propose the following situation: a store manager (played by you or another volunteer) is speaking with two Christian employees about their reactions to the recent death of Sally, a young coworker. The employees will look for opportunities to talk about their Christian faith in the conversation.

The store manager will initiate the conversation with positive comments on the commitment of the employees to their jobs, compliment the ways they handled the problems during Sally's recent illness, and make note of the care and concern they have shown to Sally's family before and after Sally's funeral. Ask why they behaved as they did. Make lighthearted comments that their involvement at church must be making a difference in their lives. Ask questions about Christianity and un-Christian beliefs. Use Resource Page 1A to frame other questions and comments. Allow the roleplay to run for about five minutes.

Then ask the class to comment on ways they heard the three principles expressed in the volunteers' comments and responses. Did they hear words spoken in love and statements of the Gospel? How did the employees stay alert for temptations to be led astray? How did this exercise compare to real life situations? What would others have said in a different way? Expect a variety of answers and affirm participants for offering comments.

Closing Prayer

Ask if any participants have friends that need to know Jesus Christ who could be included in the prayer. Also invite other special prayer requests. Then offer the petitions in a prayer you create, or use the following: "Dear Savior, You paid an incredible price for each one of us. You gave Your life so that we can spend eternity with You. Thank You for Your love and constant care. We know other people who need Your salvation too. Send Your Holy Spirit into the hearts of (list the names). Use us to tell them Your story of love. Be with those who are in need, including (mention their names). Give them healing of mind and body and the assurance of Your love. In Your blessed name we pray. Amen."

Christianity—A Standard for Comparison

History

The Christian church dates its beginning as Pentecost in A.D. 30, when the disciples of Jesus Christ first received the Holy Spirit and the power to preach the Good News of salvation through Jesus to all people. Though faced with persecution, the followers of Jesus spread the Gospel throughout the world. The church was essentially one body for a thousand years. A split between the East and West in 1054, the Reformation movement in the sixteenth century, and other divisions in the past 500 years have resulted in hundreds of denominations today.

Central Teaching

Christians recognize Jesus to be the *Christ* (the "anointed one" or Messiah) sent by God to redeem all people from the sinfulness that has been our nature since Adam and Eve first sinned in the Garden of Eden. Jesus is both God and man (Colossians 2:9, Isaiah 9:6, 2 John 7). Any religion that does not acknowledge Jesus as Lord and Savior is not Christian (1 John 4:1-6).

Significant People

Jesus taught 12 chosen men, and many others, about God's love and His coming kingdom. Three disciples—Peter, James, and John—received special attention from Jesus and are prominent in the early years of Christianity. Jesus performed many miracles in their presence to fulfill the Old Testament prophecies about the Messiah. Most of the 12 disciples were murdered because of their Christian faith.

The apostle Paul was converted to Christianity about five years after Jesus' death and resurrection. He became one of the greatest New Testament evangelists and brought the Christian religion to people throughout the Roman empire.

The Christian church in every age has been blessed with people who have, by God's grace, guided its teachings and mission. Even a lengthy list would be woefully incomplete. Perhaps two names stand a little taller than the rest.

Augustine of Hippo (354-430), bishop in North Africa, provided deep spiritual leadership during a series of major controversies, including the struggle against *Pelagianism,* the notion that we in some way are able to initiate God's favor through our own will.

During the time of the Reformation, God raised up many leaders to direct His people back to the truth. Martin Luther (1483-1546)—a monk, professor, and preacher—rediscovered the Good News that we are justified by grace alone, through faith in Christ alone, as taught by Scripture alone. Many others joined in similar reform efforts throughout Europe.

Other Major Teachings

The Christian church, confessing God's truth on the basis of Scripture, is united by many common beliefs, including:

- The Trinity—one God who is three persons—Father, Son, and Holy Spirit.
- The Bible—God has revealed Himself through the 66 books of the Old and New Testament by inspiring those who wrote them.
- Sin—Both a condition of our hearts and our wrongful actions, sin is universal to human beings—"all have sinned" (Romans 3:23)—and results in every heartache, corruption, sickness, and death.
- Law—God has made His will known to us both by writing it "on our hearts" (Romans 2:15)—that is, our conscience—and making it clear through His Word, the Bible. The Law is not limited to God's commandments, but is taught in every Scripture that shows us His will for our lives.
- Gospel—The Good News of God's abundant love toward His whole creation. Because God loves us, He gives us forgiveness of sins and eternal life through the work of His Son Jesus, that is, by grace through faith in Jesus as our Savior, without any work or merit on our part.
- Eternal Life—When Christians believe in Jesus, God works new life in them through the Holy Spirit. When Christians die, God brings them into His presence to spend eternity in heaven.
- The Sacraments—These are the tools God gives the church, commanded by Jesus, through which His words with common elements (the water of Baptism and the bread and wine of Holy Communion) work faith, forgiveness, and the assurance of eternal life.

Contemporary Encounter

Nearly a third of the world's population (about two billion people) describe themselves as Christian, more than any other religion. Although the Christian church is known today in hundreds of denominations that vary in their beliefs and practices, it is united in the basic doctrines of belief in the triune God, reliance on the Bible as God's Word, and salvation through Jesus Christ alone.

Christian Connection

Central to the Christian faith is the belief that Jesus, God's only Son, is both fully human and fully divine. For the wrong things we have done, Jesus lived a life of *passive obedience*. He suffered and died so that we might receive God's gift of forgiveness of sins and be called God's forgiven children. For the good things we have failed to do, Jesus lived a life of *active obedience*. He fulfilled all the Law so that we might receive God's gift of Christ's righteousness and be called saints of God.

Scripture quotation: NIV®. Used by permission of Zondervan.

The Heart of the Gospel

> [6] So then, just as you received Christ Jesus as Lord, continue to live in Him, rooted and built up in Him, [7] strengthened in the faith as you were taught, and overflowing with thankfulness. [8] See to it that no one takes you captive through hollow and deceptive philosophy, which depends on human tradition and the basic principles of this world rather than on Christ.
>
> [9] For in Christ all the fullness of the Deity lives in bodily form, [10] and you have been given fullness in Christ, who is the head over every power and authority. [11] In Him you were also circumcised, in the putting off of the sinful nature, not with a circumcision done by the hands of men but with the circumcision done by Christ, [12] having been buried with Him in baptism and raised with Him through your faith in the power of God, who raised Him from the dead. (Colossians 2:6–12)

1. The apostle Paul writes in Colossians to Christians who, like the Christian church today, are under attack by those with false teachings. Paul points them—and us—to Christ and all that He provides. In verses 6–7, underline the verbs and verb-forms that point us to Christ. What do each of them teach us about our relationship with Christ?

2. Paul says that "hollow and deceptive philosophy" depends on "human tradition and the basic principles of this world" rather than on Christ. What are some examples of such hollow traditions and worldly principles?

3. Christ is sufficient for us, says Paul, because the fullness of God (the totality of God with all His powers and attributes) is in Him. What specific powers and attributes of God that we see in Jesus are most important to our life now and eternally?

4. Finally, Paul affirms our fullness in Christ—we have everything we need in Him. What specifics does Paul describe in verses 11–12? Why are they important to you?

Scripture quotation is NIV®. Used by permission of Zondervan.

How Would You Respond?

Bible Study Leader: If you plan to use small groups for this activity, make a copy of this page for every three small groups you anticipate and separate the three case studies for easy distribution.

Case Study 1

You have discovered that a new neighbor is not a Christian. In fact, he seems to be somewhat antagonistic toward Christianity. In a casual conversation, he makes the following comment: "I've heard that Christians don't get along. I mean, look at all the different denominations right here in our neighborhood. Can't you people agree on anything?"

How would you respond?

Case Study 2

A favorite cousin will be spending her next year of college studying in China. At a family gathering, you are talking with her in the kitchen. She says: "I understand that the Christian churches in China are not allowed to represent different denominations. That's okay, I guess, but how should I choose a church in which to worship while I'm there? What questions should I ask? What should I look for?"

How would you respond?

Case Study 3

Two young friends are seeing each other and talking about marriage. One of them is a member of your church, the other is of another denomination. You are eating together one evening when they ask you: "Do you think it is important for us to be members of the same church if we are married? Why should one of us have to change churches? All Christian churches believe the same basic things anyway, don't they?"

How would you respond?

One God, Many Gods   **Resource Page 1C**   © 1998 CPH

Judaism
The Descendants of Abraham

Isaiah 61:1–2; Luke 7:18–23

Study Outline: Judaism

Activity	Time Suggested	Materials Needed
Opening Activities (Choose one)		
Trip to Nowhere	15 minutes	Sets of clues
Holy Days	10 minutes	Newsprint or marker board and markers
Studying the Word		
Review of Judaism	10 minutes	Copies of Resource Page 2A
God Speaks, God Acts	15 minutes	Copies of Resource Page 2B, Bibles, pencils or pens
Applying the Word (Choose one)		
Speaking the Truth	15 minutes	Blank paper
A Point to Ponder	10 minutes	
Closing Prayer	5 minutes	Songbooks (optional)

Opening Activities

Choose one of the following activities, but not both, unless you have extra time.

Trip to Nowhere

Write each of the five clues on a separate index card or piece of paper. On each card also include directions to the next clue. (The first clue should direct them to a point outside the classroom. The final clue should direct the searchers back to the starting point in the classroom.) Before class, place clues 2–5 carefully—clue 2 at the location named on clue 1, etc. Bring the first clue to class.

Clue 1   This religion traces its roots to a herdsman who lived around 2,000 B.C. *Find the next clue …*

Clue 2   The followers of this religion hold strictly to laws given them by God. *Find the next clue …*

Clue 3   The followers of this religion maintain that God has promised them a particular land and to this day they are willing to fight for it. *Find the next clue …*

Clue 4   Only once in history have these people been a world power. The king who built that empire is still revered to this day. *Find the next clue …*

Clue 5   In spite of persecution and exile, these people continue to be a major political force in the world today. *Find the "treasure" back in the classroom.*

Focus

Of all other religions, Christianity finds its closest kinship with Judaism. Jesus and His disciples were Jews. Jesus lived and ministered in Israel. Jesus went to Jerusalem, the holy city of Judaism, for the major religious festivals.

We share with Judaism many beliefs, including the authenticity and divine authority of the Old Testament, faith in the one true God, and hope in the Messiah and resurrection. But most Jews do not yet share our faith in Jesus as the fulfillment of the Old Testament prophecies for the Messiah and the source of salvation from our sin.

Objectives

The participants, through the study of God's Word and the power of the Holy Spirit, will

1. identify the common and contrasting beliefs of Christians and Jews;
2. recognize Jesus Christ as the promised Messiah and their Savior from sin;
3. give thanks for the mercy they receive from God through His Son.

Advance Preparation Required

A quick way to prepare the clues for this activity is to photocopy them as they appear on this page, one copy for every four or five

participants. Then add the
directions, separate the clues,
and place them for the treasure hunt. You can adapt this
activity to indoor or outdoor
situations.

If you are working with a
group of adults, you might
wish to read the clues. It
shouldn't take very long to
guess the religion described,
but share all the clues anyway. Each clue will serve to
underscore the close parallels
between Christianity and
Judaism.

You may wish to have the
participants record their
guesses on scrap paper. Or
you may wish to allow group
discussion and choices.

Introduce the activity by saying, "You are going on a treasure hunt.
Through a series of clues, the religion we will study today will be
revealed. The clues will lead to your destination where you will learn
about a treasure." Give the participants clue 1, instructing them to find
and follow the other four clues.

The participants will arrive back at the classroom. Ask them what religion they think they will be studying. Point out that the treasure hunt
ended at its beginning and failed to lead to a treasure. Remind them
that the Old Testament Jews were on a 2,000-year journey. Jesus—
God's promised Messiah and treasure—arrived right in their midst but
they missed Him. To this day many Jews are still expecting the Messiah
who has already come.

Holy Days

*Use this activity or the previous one, but not both, unless you have
extra time.*

List these Jewish religious festivals on a sheet of newsprint or on the
board, *in a different order than shown.* Read aloud the numbered
summaries without naming the festivals. Challenge the participants to
match the summaries and festivals.

Hanukkah	1.	An eight-day festival of lights commemorating the reclaiming of the temple in Jerusalem in 164 B.C. (mid-December).
Passover	2.	A seven-day festival celebrating deliverance from the Egyptians through the Red Sea (March-April).
Weeks	3.	A harvest festival that commemorates the giving of the Law on Mount Sinai (May-June). Also called Pentecost.
Trumpets	4.	Trumpets are blown to usher in a civil new year (September-October). Later called *Rosh Hashanah.*
Yom Kippur	5.	A day of rest, confession, and fasting for reconciliation between God and people. In ancient Israel, this day included a sacrifice of atonement for sin (September-October).
Tabernacles	6.	A feast commemorating the 40 years of wandering in the wilderness and the ingathering of the harvest that once involved living in tabernacles (tent-like booths) (September-October).
Purim	7.	The feast of Esther, celebrating the deliverance of the Israelites during the Babylonian exile (February-March).

Studying the Word

Use both of the following activities if possible.

Review of Judaism

As an alternative, divide the
class into small groups. Ask
each group to read the summary and develop a list of
questions that they would ask

Distribute copies of Resource Page 2A and say, "Judaism has a long history with roots back to Abraham. It is a tradition that Christians can
identify with, since it is recorded in the Old Testament."

Ask for volunteers to read aloud the sections of the resource page. Then ask, "What kinds of questions might you ask an expert on Judaism?" These questions will be left unanswered. They may move some to personal study. If so, invite them to share their findings briefly at the next session.

God Speaks, God Acts

Distribute copies of Resource Page 2B, "God Speaks, God Acts." Old Testament prophecies and their New Testament fulfillments are listed. Participants will summarize the individual prophecies and their fulfillments. Participants can work in their small groups, with a partner or individually on the worksheet. You will need to allow at least 15 minutes for the participants to complete the assignment.

The prophecies are:

- Genesis 12:1–3, 7   The covenant with Abraham includes the promise of the Messiah.

- Genesis 49:10   The Messiah would come from the tribe of Judah.

- Deuteronomy 8:15–19   He would be a prophet like Moses.

- Isaiah 7:14   He would be born of a virgin.

- Micah 5:2   He would be born in Bethlehem.

- Jeremiah 31:31–34   He would institute a new covenant.

- Isaiah 61:1–2   He would relieve the ills of God's people.

- Isaiah 52:13, 53:3–12   The Messiah is described as a suffering servant.

- Jonah 1:17–2:10   He would be resurrected after three days.

After 15 minutes, or when the participants have completed the assignment, review the resource page with the class. Then discuss the prophecies using the following questions.

1. What common themes did you sense in God's promises about the Messiah? (God loves His people and desires to redeem them.)

2. What evidence is there that Jesus was indeed the promised Messiah? (Jesus fulfilled all of the prophecies.)

3. How is it possible that the Jews missed the message? (Jesus did not fit what many expected of the Messiah).

Applying the Word (Choose one)

Speaking the Truth

Use this activity or the one that follows, but not both, unless you have extra time.

Introduce this activity by saying, "While many Jews reject Jesus as the promised Messiah, our common heritage provides grounds on which to begin to share our faith with them. In this portion of the lesson, we will develop a presentation of the Good News. Many Jews still stress obedience to the Law. Our presentation should point out that full obedience to the Law is not possible. In the end, salvation is only found in Jesus."

an expert on Judaism if they had the opportunity. Provide each group with a sheet of newsprint paper on which to record at least three questions for all to see.

To Shorten This Activity

To make this exercise easier and spend less time searching out Bible passages, provide the participants with the Old Testament prophesy descriptions, either by reading them aloud or by writing them on the Resource Page before creating the copies. Focus on the New Testament passages that fulfill the prophecies.

To Go Deeper

Some groups may be familiar with most of the prophecies listed in this exercise. It may be helpful to focus on the Isaiah 61:1–2 passage (see also Isaiah 29:18–19 and 35:5–6). Each of these passages focuses on the "Messianic Age"—the time beginning with the Messiah's first coming to save us and ending with His return in glory and judgment at the end of time. Jesus applies these prophecies directly to Himself in Luke 4:14–21 and the Luke 7 passage. Jesus also demonstrates the actions listed in Mark's gospel (the blind see—10:46–52; the lame walk—2:3–12; leprosy is cured—1:40–42; the deaf hear—7:31–37; Good News is preached—1:14–15) and many other places.

Encourage participants to use the passages found on Resource Page 2B in developing their presentation. Remind them that Paul's letter to the Romans was written to Jews and Gentiles living in Roman with the intent of sharing the Gospel with *both!* In Romans 4, Paul builds a case for the fact that Abraham was saved through his faith in the promise of God. You also will want to display the following references as additional passages they might use: Romans 3:21–24, Romans 7:7–25 (specifically verses 7b, and 14).

Give the participants 10 minutes to work. Then invite volunteers to share their presentations.

Remind the participants that actual evangelistic efforts among the Jews can be very difficult. To be effective we must first demonstrate respect for Jewish people and their traditions. Ask, "What are some ways that we can be effective building a relationship with Jews?" (Possible responses include respecting their holy days and festivals, showing an interest in their holiday traditions, refraining from using any ethnic expression or humor that belittles Jews.)

A Resource

How to Respond: Judaism, Erwin Kolb, CPH, 1995.

A Point to Ponder

Use this activity or the previous one, but not both, unless you have extra time.

Write the following thought on the board or on newsprint: "Jesus can only be seen clearly as the Messiah in the Old Testament with eyes of faith." Ask the participants what that statement means to them.

During the discussion that follows, make these observations. "We as Christians have the benefit of faith given us by God through the Holy Spirit as we study the Old and the New Testament. It's like solving a puzzle when someone has already shown you the solution. We believe in Jesus and, therefore, see the prophecies that point to Him in the Old Testament. We cannot expect that, on the basis of logical argument alone, anyone will come to faith in Jesus Christ as the Messiah. Only the Holy Spirit working through God's Word can create faith. But we *can* share that Word with people, including our Jewish friends and neighbors. We can let them see our faith and share with them how it makes a difference in our lives.

Closing Devotions

As part of the closing devotion, sing one or more songs that reflect both Jewish culture and the Gospel message. Examples might be "King of Kings and Lord of Lords" (*All God's People Sing* 151) or "El Shaddai" (*AGPS* 92).

Close the session with the following prayer: "Loving Father, through the Old Testament patriarchs and prophets, You revealed Your plan of salvation. Help us use our knowledge of that history to build relationships with those who are still looking for the Messiah. Through our words and actions, help us share our faith with them so that they might see the hope that can be found only in Jesus Christ. Through the power of Your Holy Spirit, may that be accomplished through us. Amen."

Judaism—the Descendants of Abraham

History

Judaism traces its roots back to Abraham in 2,000 B.C. God's promises to Abraham (Genesis 12:1–3) and His covenant (Genesis 15:1–21) begin the relationship between God and the Jews.

In the nineteenth century, Judaism divided into three groups—orthodox, conservative, and reformed. Teachings vary widely among these groups, with Reformed Judaism allowing significant departures from the traditional Jewish beliefs expressed in this summary.

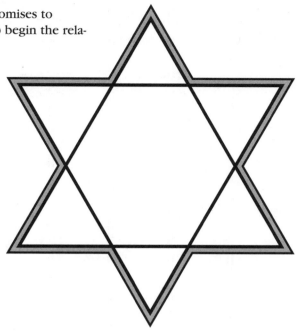

Central Teaching

God is a personal, all-powerful, eternal, and compassionate God. His history with His people and His basic teachings are found in the Torah, the first five books of the Old Testament. Judaism also accepts as true the entire Old Testament and the Talmud, a 2,700-page record of the teachings of ancient rabbis.

Significant People

In addition to Abraham, the other Old Testament patriarchs—Isaac, Jacob, Moses, and others—are considered giants of the faith. King David is also revered because under him Israel became a mighty world power.

Other Major Teachings

Judaism stresses obedience to the Law (the Ten Commandments). While they acknowledge the necessity of God's mercy since no one can perfectly keep the Law, they do not acknowledge the substitutionary sacrifice of Jesus. Atonement for sin is made through works of righteousness, prayer, and repentance. Many Jews believe in a physical resurrection. Judaism does not accept Jesus Christ as the promised Messiah. To Jews he is either a false prophet or, a martyred teacher. Orthodox Jews believe the true Messiah is still to come. The Messiah's arrival will mean the restoration of the Jewish nation and His physical rule on the earth.

Contemporary Encounters

There are around six million Jews living in the United States. A majority of these are practicing Jews. Almost every major city has at least one Jewish synagog. Jewish people are very visible in our culture. In the entertainment industry, individuals such as Steven Spielberg and Barbara Streisand are practicing Jews. Jews can be found among the leaders in the fields of government, science, and business.

Christian Connection

We share many common beliefs with Judaism. Most Jews will be familiar with Jesus, but they won't acknowledge Him as the Savior. Because of their belief that the Messiah has not yet come, we can witness to Jews by celebrating the hope we have in Jesus. An active, dynamic faith that openly confesses Jesus is the best witness.

God Speaks, God Acts

Old Testament Promise	Prophecy	New Testament Fulfillment
Genesis 12:1-3, 7		Romans 9:4-5
Genesis 49:10		Matthew 1
Deuteronomy 18:15-19		Acts 3:19-23
Isaiah 7:14		Matthew 1:18-20
Micah 5:2		Matthew 2:1-6
Jeremiah 31:31-34		Hebrews 8:1-13
Isaiah 61:1-2		Luke 7:18-23
Isaiah 52:13, 53:3-12		John 19:28-30
Jonah 1:17-2:10		Matthew 12:39-40; 16:4, 21

One God, Many Gods   **Resource Page 2B**   © 1998 CPH

Hinduism
Striving for Moksha
Hebrews 9:27–28

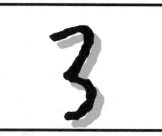

Study Outline: Hinduism

Activity	Time Suggested	Materials Needed
Opening Activity		
Agree or Not	10 minutes	
Studying the Word		
About Hinduism	15 minutes	Copies of Resource Page 3A; Bibles
Exposing the Truth	15 minutes	Copies of Resource Page 3B; Bibles
Applying the Word		
Meditating on God's Word	10 minutes	Index cards with Scripture references
Right Things for the Right Reason	5 minutes	(Also on Resource Page 3B)
Closing Prayer	5 minutes	

Opening Activity

Agree or Not

Have all participants stand behind a marked or imaginary line. Read the following statements. If, as Christians, the participants agree with a statement, they remain where they are. If they disagree, they step over the line. If they are unsure, or if they think the statement is too vague, they stand on the line. (Less active groups may be more comfortable simply raising hands to indicate agreement, diagreement, or uncertainty.)

Do you believe …

1. in showing respect toward others, especially your elders?
2. in showing respect toward animals and other living things?
3. that your words and actions bring about consequences?
4. that individuals create their own destiny?
5. that words and actions will result in a better status when one is reincarnated into the next life?
6. that a person can make payment for past sins through suffering in the next life?

Most participants will probably agree, that as Christians, the first three points are important. (You may note, though, that for Christians these beliefs come as a result of God's gift of faith in us; they do not earn salvation.) Christians usually do not choose to use the word *destiny* (statement 4.) when speaking about the future. According to Scripture, God is

Focus

The Hindu road to salvation is a circular path of works by which the soul is repeatedly reborn—with more good and less evil in each life, it is hoped—until the soul is liberated from fleshly existence to be entirely one with Brahman. To those mired in personal effort and at the mercy of <u>karma</u>, our loving God offers the merits of His own Son Jesus Christ, a single life of faith and service, and the joy of a guaranteed eternity with Him when we die.

Objectives

The participants, through the study of God's Word and the power of the Holy Spirit, will

1. review the basic teachings of Hinduism;
2. recognize the danger of self-righteousness;
3. rejoice in a God who loves them and offers the free gift of salvation.

Behind the Symbol
(An Optional Opening Activity)

Before class, draw a swastika symbol on a piece of newsprint and post it on the wall. As class begins, ask the participants what comes to mind when they see the symbol. (Many participants may think of events associated with World War II and the Hitler regime.) Explain that the Germans did not invent this symbol. The swastika is a symbol in India that means "bringing health." The Hindu religion uses the swastika as a sign of good fortune and protection against evil.

Discuss Christian symbols and what they mean, as well as how non-Christians might interpret them.

This example of Hindu influence was found in a community education flyer: "Health and Fitness through Yoga—This class is a survey of yogic breathing, vinyasa, classification, cariation, and adaptation of asanas, and their relationship to athletics, dance, posture, and therapy. The course is inspired by the teachings of T. Krishnamacharya (Krishna as part of a name indicates a follower of Vishnu, the god of preservation) and T. K. V. Desikachar. It is a tremendous introduction to yoga, and is ideal for advanced students as well."

in control so that all things may ultimately work out for His purposes. It is true, however, that God allows us to act upon situations and make decisions. Because of our sinful nature, we do not always do the right things, and our actions bring about certain consequences. Christians must disagree with points 5 and 6. Scripture teaches that people will die only once and that Christ has made the once-for-all payment for our sins. Hebrews 9:27–28 says, "Just as man is destined to die once, and after that to face judgment, so Christ was sacrificed once to take away the sins of many people; and He will appear a second time, not to bear sin, but to bring salvation to those who are waiting for Him."

Say, "Today we will be looking at the Hindu religion. As with many religions, there are some things we can agree with in Hinduism. However, there are critical points with which Christians must disagree."

Studying the Word
About Hinduism

Distribute copies of Resource Page 3A. Read aloud, or have volunteers read aloud, sections of the page. Have the class put a star next to those things which are new or of interest to them for discussion later. The majority of Hindus are found in India, with 83 percent of the population being Hindu. Yet, Hinduism has affected all parts of the world. In particular, its popular off-shoots, Transcendental Meditation and Hare Krishna movement, have gained many followers in North America. (Resources for additional study are noted toward the end of this chapter.)

Exposing the Truth

Distribute copies of Resource Page 3B and direct the participants to the first section of the page. The statements printed there are true for Hindus, but not for Christians. If your class has more than five participants, you may want to have them work in small groups or pairs. Have each individual or group look up the Scripture references and write a statement that counters the Hindu belief. Samples of such statements are:

1. There is only one God—the the Father, Son, and Holy Spirit.
2. Jesus is true God, the third Person in the Trinity, one with the Father.
3. Christ took our sins upon Himself so that we could be forgiven.
4. God forbids us to worship idols; these images can do us no good.
5. Salvation is a gift of God. We do not become God, but we become heirs of His righteousness and blessings.
6. We are not able to assist in our salvation. Those who have faith are moved by the Spirit to live a new life.
7. We die only once.

Point out that there are clear differences between Christianity and Hinduism. These distinctions are important to our understanding of, and ability to witness to, those of the Hindu faith.

Applying the Word

Meditating on God's Word

Before class, write the following Scripture references on index cards.

Romans 8:31-39—For those who desire a deeper faith or who are struggling with anxiety or stress

Psalm 9:9-10—For those who want to feel less stressed out

Psalm 103:9-12—For those who want to know they're forgiven

Isaiah 41:10-13—For those struggling with anxiety/stress

Matthew 6:25-34—For those struggling with worry

1 Corinthians 13:4-8—For those struggling with anger or learning to show love

Ephesians 4:22-24—For those struggling to live as Christians

1 Peter 1:3-5—For those struggling to hold on to hope

1 John 3:11-20—For those struggling with bitterness or learning to forgive

Explain to the participants that meditation exercises can be beneficial for Christians—emotionally, physically, and spiritually. The key is on *whom* we focus our meditation. Christian meditation focuses on the triune God. Therefore, meditation exercises often include reading Scripture, confession, and prayer—allowing the Holy Spirit to speak to us and to help us respond by obedience. Assign each participant one of the passages or allow them to select one. Have them look up the passage and read it through at least two times to themselves. Then ask them to share what message of peace, direction, strength, or comfort they find in that passage.

Encourage participants to take the Scripture reference home and read it at the beginning of each day that week. Also, encourage them to talk to God about the feelings, ideas, and questions they may have related to the passage.

Close by saying, "Hindus believe that through meditation they become more enlightened to the truth, and thus become one with God. Christians realize, though, that those who do not confess Jesus as Savior, are really in darkness, no matter how hard they may try to be enlightened. It says in 2 Corinthians 4:4, 'The god of this age has blinded the minds of unbelievers, so that they cannot see the light of the Gospel of the glory of Christ.' Thanks be to God that through the work of the Holy Spirit, you and I know the Light of the World, Jesus Christ, as the Way, the Truth and the Life."

Right Things for the Right Reason

Remind the participants that, though Hindus believe that they must strive to lead good lives in order to achieve salvation, Christians believe that salvation becomes ours as a gift. The gift of faith is something that the Holy Spirit works in us. Faith means trusting that our salvation was won for us by Jesus, apart from anything we could ever do.

Resources

The Hindu Connection, A. R. Victor Raj, CPH, 1995

World Religions: Hinduism, Dilip Kadodwala, Thomson Learning, New York, 1995

How to Become a Hindu, © 1996 Himalayan Academy, www.hinduismtoday.kauai.hi. us/Himalayan Academy/ Publications/JnanaDana/ BecomeHindu.html

A Christian's obedience to God is a consequence of what God has already done for us. Unfortunately, our sinful nature gets in the way sometimes, and we do things because "we have to" or because we're afraid we might otherwise get in trouble.

Direct participants to this section of Resource Page 3B. Have them think of three things that they can do to show respect for other people or things and write their ideas in the boxes, list "not so good" reasons for doing these things, and good reasons to do these things—reasons that reflect their faith. Say, "As a Christian, the Holy Spirit will keep working in you as your faith is nurtured through the Word and sacraments. Remember that the Holy Spirit is there to give you strength to obey God, assure you of God's forgiveness when you fail, and give you joy because He will complete His work in you. We will be made perfect when we stand face to face with God in heaven someday, all because of God's work for and in us."

Closing Prayer

Close the study with a prayer like this one: "Dear heavenly Father, forgive our efforts to earn Your approval, and our complete failure to do so. Move us by Your Holy Spirit to rely on and live in Your love. In Jesus' name we pray. Amen."

Hinduism—Striving for Moksha

History

One of the world's oldest religions, Hinduism developed between 1800–1000 B.C. in India. Hinduism contains many sects. Hinduism is both a religion and a way of life. It is described in the *Vedas* (considered the world's most ancient scriptures, about 1000 B.C.) and the *Bhagavad-Gita*, an 18-chapter poem.

Central Teaching

Hindus believe that all things are part of God, that souls are reincarnated at death, and that our lives are influenced by *karma* (good and bad actions in this life determine one's status in the next). The goal is *moksha*, release from the cycle of reincarnation to become one with God.

Significant People

Hinduism developed over many centuries; there is no single significant founder or leader. The most famous among its followers is Mahatma Gandhi, who led India to freedom from the British Empire in the early twentieth century.

Other Major Teachings

1. *Brahman* is the "Absolute," present everywhere and in everything. Hindus acknowledge a "trinity"—*Brahma* (god of creation), *Shiva* (god of destruction), and *Vishnu* (god of preservation).
2. *Karma*—Individuals creates their own destinies.
3. Souls evolve through many reincarnations—good people to a better state; evil people to lives of suffering.
4. In any life, one's place is fixed in a *caste* or level of society.
5. Moksha can be achieved through yoga and meditation.
6. A *guru*, a spiritually awakened teacher, helps guide a person toward total realization of God.
7. Other important beliefs are personal discipline, purification, pilgrimages to sacred places, religious study, temple worship, observation of holy days, and rites of passage at significant times of life.
8. New Hindus observe a name-giving sacrament. New names reflect the names of gods or indicate one's caste and sect. Hindu names may change more than once in their lifetime as a result of a blessing at a temple or other spiritual events.
9. All life is sacred and should be respected and not harmed.
10. No particular religion teaches the only way to salvation above all others. All genuine religious paths are facets of God's "pure love and light" and deserve tolerance.

Contemporary Encounters

The New Age movement and Transcendental Meditation are popular movements founded on Hinduism. Meditation and yoga have become common forms of stress release in our society with classes offered at local colleges and fitness centers. Many celebrities have been attracted to Hinduism, such as George Harrison of the Beatles, who donated proceeds from record sales to the Hare Krishna Movement (a sect of Hinduism).

Christian Connection

According to God's Word, salvation is found only in the saving work of the Triune God (Acts 4:12). Although Christians are to live in obedience to God, their salvation is not dependent on this (Ephesians 2:8–9).

Exposing the Truth

The statements below are true for Hindus, but not for Christians. Look up the Scripture references to help you find out the truth that shows each Hindu belief to be false.

1. Hindus believe that people are God but unaware of it. (1 Corinthians 8:4b–6)

2. Jesus is a teacher, a *guru* or an *avatar* (an incarnation of the god Vishnu.) (1 John 5:20)

3. Jesus' death does not pay for anyone's sins but His own. We are all responsible for paying for our own sins. (1 Peter 2:24)

4. Hindus worship idols because these images are the incarnations of the invisible gods. (Exodus 20:3-5; Jeremiah 10:5)

5. Through meditation and a good karma, a person must strive to become united with the gods and thus achieve salvation. (Ephesians 2:8-9)

6. Some of Hindu off-shoots, such as yoga and meditation, are innocent and beneficial for salvation. (Ephesians 5:6; 2 Peter 3:17)

7. The soul is reincarnated and a person may live many lives before achieving moksha. (Hebrews 9:27-28)

Right Things for the Right Reason

Inside the boxes, write three things that you could do that would show respect or kindness. What are some good reasons to do these things? Write them in the box along with the action.

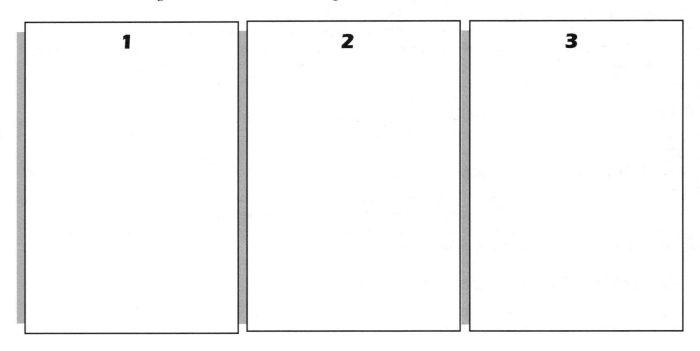

1	2	3

One God, Many Gods

Resource Page 3B

Buddhism
The Eightfold Path
John 14:6

Study Outline: Buddhism

Activity	Time Suggested	Materials Needed
Opening Activities (Choose one)		
Erasing Sin?	10 minutes	Newsprint, permanent markers, erasers, correction fluid, masking tape
One Way	5 minutes	Combination lock
Studying the Word		
Four Noble Truths	15 minutes	Bibles, newsprint or marker board, markers, copies of Resource Page 4A
The Eightfold Path	15 minutes	Bibles; copies of Resource Page 4B
Applying the Word		
Remaining in Him	10 minutes	Copies of Resource Page 4B
Closing Prayer	5 minutes	

Opening Activities

Erasing Sin?

Use this activity or the one that follows, but not both, unless you have extra time.

On a large sheet of newsprint draw an outline of a person. Inside the person draw a number of black marks with a permanent marker. Provide variety of erasers, masking tape, correction fluid, and other things to erase or cover the marks. Invite volunteers to erase or cover up the black marks. After several volunteers have worked to undo the marks, compliment their efforts. However, point out that though the marks might be hidden from sight, they are not gone. The only way to have a perfectly clean drawing again is to start with a new one.

Ask your class, "How is this like the way many people deal with sin in their lives?" (We do all kinds of things to try to cover up our sin, but we can never really get rid of it.) Point out that this is true of all non-Christian religions including Buddhism.

One Way

Use this activity or the previous one, but not both, unless you have extra time.

Display a combination lock. Challenge one or more of the participants to open the lock without providing the combination. After allowing the participants to give it a try ask, "How many combinations will open this lock?" (Just one.) Demonstrate the actual combination.

Point out that the combination is a fact. No amount of sincere belief in, or fervent desire that the lock open with, another combination can change that fact. You could know the real combination, read it from the instructions, accidentally stumble across it, or be told it, but you must have that one combination to open the lock. It's the way the lock is designed. In the same way, God has chosen a way to reveal Himself to us so that we might know Him. In John 14:6, Jesus says, "I am the way and the truth and the life. No one comes to the Father except through Me." One combination: to the Father through the Son.

Studying the Word

Use both of the following activities.

Four Noble Truths

Before class write the "Four Noble Truths" from Resource Page 4A under "Other Major Teachings" on newsprint or on the board. Leave enough space in between the lines so you can cross out some words and add others.

Distribute copies of Resource Page 4A. Ask volunteers to read aloud through the sections of the worksheet. Stop when you reach the "Four Noble Truths." Explain that you want the class to examine these "truths" more closely in light of the Bible. If they are false, you will rewrite them to make them true. Ask a volunteer to make the rewrites on the newsprint or marker board as the class suggests changes. Use these comments in the discussion:

1. This one is basically true. The world is full of all kinds of suffering—see Job 14:1; Ecclesiastes 2:23. Some might argue with the words "is full;" if so, change them to "has lots of."

2. This one could be true or false. Challenge the participants to think of Bible passages to support their response. (James 1:14–15 might suggest the second noble truth is correct. Romans 7:21–25 says that we are slaves to our sinful nature. This is more than just selfish desires. It is a condition, a state of being. In this sense, this "noble truth" is false. Revelation 12:9 reminds us that Satan is at work in the world causing pain and misery.) This truth could be rewritten, *"This misery and suffering are caused by our selfish desires as a result of original sin* and *the active involvement of Satan in the world."*

3. Will getting rid of selfish desires eliminate misery and suffering? Yes and no. If suffering was caused *only* by our selfish desires, then the solution would be to get rid of selfish desires as this "truth" proposes. However, point out that if drowning people could save themselves they wouldn't be drowning. In our sinful state, we are drowning in an ocean of sin. We need a rescuer. Ask someone to read 1 John 5:4–5. Then ask, "What does this say about how we

Resources

An excellent resource for additional study on Buddhist beliefs and practices is <u>Handbook of Today's Religions</u> by Josh McDowell and Don Stewart published by Thomas Nelson Publishers.

Many Buddhism sites exist on the Internet. Use your favorite search engine to locate more background information.

overcome misery and suffering?" (It is overcome through faith in God's Son.) Now help the class rewrite noble truth number 3. It should look something like this: *"Misery and suffering can be eliminated only through the total victory Jesus Christ has won through His death and resurrection."*

4. Direct the participants to scan the eightfold path from Resource Page 4A. Ask their reactions. Point out that there is nothing here that addresses our need for rescue. Buddhism relies on what we *do.* But our problem is not just impure thoughts or lack of spiritual knowledge. We are drowning, totally incapable of helping ourselves (Ephesians 2:1). Without a total change, an entirely new nature, we will perish (2 Corinthians 5:17). That change comes through what Jesus has done—and continues to do—for us.

Ask someone to read John 15:4-11. John points out that we become fruitful—that is we experience the full, joyful life that God intends, free from misery, as we "remain in Jesus, the vine." The last truth should be rewritten to look something like this: *"Jesus' victory is experienced in our lives as we remain in Him."*

The Eightfold Path

Distribute copies of Resource Page 4B. Explain that the Eightfold Path includes principles that can be found in the Bible. But God's Word does not list them as the way to heaven. Rather, they are part of the new life we have through Jesus Christ because of the victory He has already won for us. Challenge the participants to match the number of each step on the eightfold path with its scriptural counterpart, writing a brief summary of what the Bible passage says. Give the participants seven or eight minutes to match the two lists. Sample answers are:

1.—e. All understanding begins with knowing God.

2.—c. Our purpose is to seek God.

3.—h. Use words which build others up.

4.—b. You shall not murder, commit adultery, or steal.

5.—f. Love your neighbor as yourself.

6.—g. Put on Christlike virtues.

7.—d. Renew your mind through God's Word.

8.—a. Be joyful, pray, and give thanks in Christ.

Remind the class that the power to follow these principles from God's Word, and thus experience the abundant life that God gives, is our faith in Jesus which is itself a gift from God. The Buddhist believes the eightfold path is the way to enlightenment, to truth, to heaven. But the eightfold path cannot take us to God, because we need more than to be enlightened—we must be saved from drowning in our sins. To all who believe by the Spirit's power in Jesus Christ and His death for us, God gives the free gift of salvation. It is by trusting in Him that we are saved, not in doing the right things.

Take a few moments to read or have a volunteer read the remaining sections of the resource page.

If you have a larger class, ask the participants to work together in twos or threes to complete this matching assignment. For a smaller class, you might do this as a group or have the participants work individually.

Applying the Word

Remaining in Him

Ask the participants, "What do you think people find attractive about the Buddhist faith?" (Answers will vary; be affirming of all reasonable answers.) Point out that some people may turn to Buddhism for its mystical experience. They are unmoved by the traditional practice of Christianity and stop seeking God. Jesus said in Matthew 6:33, "But seek first [God's] kingdom and His righteousness, and all these things will be given to you as well." The invitation is to keep on seeking, to grow deeper in our knowledge and understanding of the new life we have in Jesus. The Holy Spirit through God's Word calls us to this search.

Then ask, "What can we as Christians learn from Buddhism that might help us in our Christian faith?" Read John 15:9–11. Point out that most people have a desire to *feel* God's presence, to *experience* Him. Explain that God has given us ways to experience Him more fully and "remaining in Him"—studying His Word, celebrating our Baptism into His death and resurrection, sharing in the forgiveness He gives in the Lord's Supper, talking with Him in prayer, and living the new life He gives through the Spirit. Explain that God's desire is that we might always know His love for us, and that He strengthens us to walk in His ways and obey His commands. Then say, "Look again at the scriptural counterparts to the steps in the eightfold path. As you look these over, which one or two stand out to you as ways God might be calling you to remain in Him?" Tell your class to fill in the blank at the bottom of the resource page with something they feel God might be calling them to do to remain in Him. For example, a participant might list "praying more" or "putting You first."

Closing Prayer

Conclude by having the participants pray, either for themselves or for each other, using the prayer they completed on the resource page.

Buddhism—the Eightfold Path

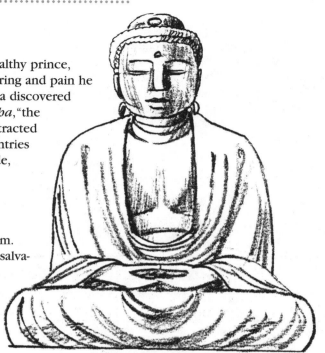

History

Buddhism arose in India about 500 B.C.. Siddartha Gautama, a wealthy prince, found that his Hindu beliefs did not adequately explain the suffering and pain he observed in the world. Through religious contemplation, Gautama discovered what he believed is the truth of life. He became known as *Buddha*, "the enlightened one," and taught others his discoveries. Buddhism attracted many followers and a variety of sects developed in different countries and cultures. Today, followers number over 300 million worldwide, about 500,000 in the United States.

Central Teaching

Pure Buddhism is more philosophy than religion, a godless pietism. Other forms of Buddhism revere Buddha as a deity and speak of salvation through faith in him. Buddhism is a journey to an enlightened state of being. People do this by accepting the *Four Noble Truths* and following the *Eightfold Path*.

Significant People

Founder: Siddartha Gautama (Buddha) about 562–480 B.C. Other major teachers: Nichiren A.D. 1222–1282 in Japan, and the Dalai Lama, currently living in exile from Tibet in Dharmasala, India.

Other Major Teachings

The Four Noble Truths: (1) life is filled with misery and suffering; (2) this misery and suffering is caused by our selfish desires; (3) misery and suffering can be eliminated by getting rid of selfish desires; and (4) these desires are eliminated by following the Eight-fold Path:

Step 1. Right views—Accept the four noble truths and the eight-fold path. *Step 2. Right thought or purpose*—Deny the pleasures of the world; do not harm any living creature nor harbor ill will toward others. *Step 3. Right speech*— Do not engage in idle talk, lying, or slander. *Step 4. Right conduct*—Do not kill any living thing; be content with what you have; be sexually pure. *Step 5. Right vocation*—Do not earn a livelihood in a way that causes anyone else harm. *Step 6. Right effort*—Get rid of negative and harmful qualities; grow in positive and helpful ones. *Step 7. Right alertness or mind control*—Be alert, observant, thoughtful, and contemplative. *Step 8. Right meditation*— Once you have abandoned sensuous desires and bad qualities, you must advance through four levels of meditation.

Contemporary Encounters

Various forms of Buddhism are gaining popularity in the U.S., especially among media and sports celebrities, including Chicago Bulls coach Phil Jackson, actor Richard Gere, and singer Tina Turner. The "middle road" and balanced life of Buddhism are a welcome change from the materialistic excesses of celebrity life.

Christian Connection

Romans 6:23—"For the wages of sin is death, but the gift of God is eternal life in Christ Jesus our Lord." Salvation is not achieved by right thoughts and right things. It is a gift given to us by a personal God through the sacrifice of His Son. We receive this gift by faith. We can never think "right enough" or do "good enough." We are saved only through Jesus' work for us.

Scripture quotation: NIV®. Used by permission of Zondervan.

The Eightfold Path

On the left are listed the eight steps of the *Eightfold Path.* Below are Scripture verses which correspond to these eight steps. Match each Scriptural truth with one of the steps and write a brief summary of the scriptural truth.

Eightfold Path	Scripture	Summary
1. Right views		
2. Right purpose		
3. Right speech		
4. Right conduct		
5. Right vocation		
6. Right effort		
7. Right alertness		
8. Right meditation		

Scriptural Truths

a. 1 Thessalonians 5:16–18

b. Exodus 20:13–15

c. Matthew 6:33

d. Romans 12:1–2

e. Proverbs 1:7

f. Galatians 5:14

g. Colossians 3:12–14

h. Ephesians 4:29

Father, thank You for saving me from sin, misery, and suffering. Help me to remain in You by _____. In Jesus' name. Amen.

Shinto
The National Worship of Japan
John 13:36–14:10

Study Outline: Shinto

Activity	Time Suggested	Materials Needed
Opening Activities		
Create a Club	15 minutes	
Truth or Not?	5 minutes	Copies of Resource Page 5A
Studying the Word		
The Way, the Truth, and the Life	15 minutes	Copies of Resource Page 5B
Applying the Word		
That's Not What the Bible Says	10 minutes	Scripture Cards (prepared from index cards)
Closing Prayer	3 minutes	

Opening Activities

Create a Club

Instruct the class that they are to create a club or exclusive organization by

1. creating a name and symbol or idol for their club;

2. creating a set of rules and rituals for club members to follow;

3. describing who leads the organization, how they become leaders, and what roles the leaders play; and

4. identifying the benefits of club membership—for the individual and for the group.

When they have finished, ask the following questions:

1. How did it feel to create your own club? (Silly, powerful, wrong.)

2. What roles did you create for yourselves in the organization? (Answers will vary.)

3. What were the most common benefits of the various organizations? What were people looking for? (Again, answers will vary, but some interesting common threads may emerge such as prosperity, happiness, and influence.)

4. What similarities did this exercise have to various religious groups today? (Perhaps none, in that the founders of religious groups rarely *set out* to create their own religions. Yet, sociologically, religious beliefs generally seek to explain life and why things happen the way they do, and in some cases religious practices seek to control things in life.)

Focus

Deeply rooted in the history and thought of the Japanese people is the belief that Japan is a divinely created country and its people descended from and are blessed by the gods. The related belief in kami, powerful spirits found in animate and inanimate objects alike, leads to the veneration of ancestors. God's Word is clear—there is only one God worthy of our worship. We are His creatures, far from divine, whom He chooses to love, forgive, and mercifully save through Christ.

Objectives

The participants, through the study of God's Word and the power of the Holy Spirit, will

1. affirm that there is only one God who is to be worshiped, served, and to whom prayers are directed;

2. confess that they are saved only through faith in Jesus Christ;

3. give thanks for their value in God's sight and the forgiveness and protection He provides through Christ.

An Option

Divide the class into groups of three or four. After about 10 minutes give the groups a chance to share their organizations with the others in the class.

Origami

Look in your local library for books that describe this unique art form (mentioned on Resource Page 5A). If you have time, provide paper and let participants try their hand at some simple designs. (As a sign of respect for the tree-spirit that gave its life for the paper, origami paper is by tradition never cut with scissors or other sharp implement. Christians may prefer to use scissors or a paper cutter.)

Divide the class into groups of three to four and have them work through the Bible study. After about 10 minutes, review the Bible study briefly with the whole class.

Then say, "Today we are going to take a look at a religion that has been around for a very long time. The religion is called Shinto. To help us learn a little more about it, we are going to take a quiz."

Truth or Not?

Challenge the participants to answer true or false to the following statements:

1. By worshiping and praying to your dead ancestors, you can receive direction for your life.
2. When you conclude a prayer you should clap your hands to get your god's attention.
3. There is not just one God but there are many spirits that are worthy of worship. These spirits can be found in trees, rivers, mountains, and rocks.
4. Faith can be based on myth and ritual, not just on a relationship with the Creator.
5. Rituals and offerings must be observed to prevent bad things from happening to you.
6. Japan was the first divine creation; the Japanese possess the ideal land and culture.

After the quiz say, "If you have answered false to any of these questions, you would not be a very good Shinto follower. All of these statements are true according to Shinto teaching."

Distribute Resource Page 5A and take a few moments to review each major section with the class. You may wish to write key words from each section on newsprint or on the board.

Studying the Word

The Way, the Truth, and the Life

Distribute copies of Resource Page 5B. Read, or have a volunteer read, the opening paragraph. Then discuss the questions, working the following comments into the discussion.

1. Jesus is preparing the disciples for His coming crucifixion and death. He will not be physically with them forever.
2. Jesus is returning to heaven by way of the cross at Calvary, the tomb, and the resurrection. He is acting out of love, fulfilling the Father's will that all people should have the opportunity for new life through faith in Christ. He does all this *for each of us*—we are the ones for whom Christ died and rose.
3. God has chosen that His Son would pay the penalty for our sins. Without that act on His part, we are condemned by our sin and separated from God forever. There is no other "name" by which we are saved (Acts 4:12).
4. Answers will vary. However, earning favor with God is ingrained into the Shinto religion. That our actions do not merit God's favor or gain us anything with God is very strange to them.

5. Shinto-believers see "god" in everything in creation. We can point out that God's creation "declares His glory" (Psalm 19:1), but His saving grace is revealed only through the loving nature and actions of His Son. We might point to Jesus' miracles, or His teaching, and certainly to His suffering, death, and resurrection for us as proof that God loves us and wants us to be with Him forever.

Applying the Word
That's Not What the Bible Says

Before class, photocopy the Bible passages at the end of this chapter on heavy paper or card stock. Separate the boxes and give each participant one or more of the Scripture cards. (In a large group, you may need more than one copy of the boxes.) Then give these instructions, "I am going to read to you some teachings of the Shinto religion. Hold up one of your Scripture cards if you think it would address that thought. There may be more than one Scripture passage to fit each topic, and some cards may be used more than once." After each reading, ask one or two volunteers to share how their Bible passage relates to that teaching. Use the following statements or others you create from topics in this lesson:

1. By worshiping and praying to your dead ancestors, you can receive direction and protection in your life.
2. Sky-Father *(Iza Nagi)* and Earth-Mother *(Iza Nami)* gave birth to the earth and that's how the world was created.
3. There is not one God but there are many spirits that are worthy of worship. These spirits can be found in trees, rivers, mountains, and rocks.
4. Faith is based upon myth and ritual, not upon a saving relationship with the Creator.
5. Rituals and offerings must be observed to prevent bad things.
6. Shinto is a nonexclusive religion, and many people practice Shinto along with a second or third religion.
7. Shinto has no real founder, no written scriptures, and no body of religious law.
8. Human beings do not rule over the earth, but are members of a community with other beings including animals, plants, minerals, and natural phenomena such as sky, water, mountains, and earth.
9. Shinto is primarily a form of nature worship.
10. Everything has a soul and a spirit including trees, mountains, animals, and buildings.

Closing Prayer

Read Ephesians 2:7–8: "In order that in the coming ages He might show the incomparable riches of His grace, expressed in His kindness to us in Christ Jesus. For it is by grace you have been saved, through faith—and this not from yourselves, it is the gift of God."

The Great Wall
Note that advanced preparation is required for this activity.

Young people and some adults will enjoy this active experience before the closing prayer.

Place a string across the room about three feet high. This is an invisible wall. On their side of the wall is nothing good, on the other side of the wall are good things. (Have a treat waiting for them, if possible.) The participants have to get from one side of the wall to the other without going under or touching the string. The whole class must get across this wall without using chairs or any other equipment. Give the group a reasonable period of time to attempt it. (Most often at least one or two will be left on the other side.) Debrief with the following questions:

1. How did it feel to be on the wrong side of the wall?
2. How did you feel trying to get to the other side?
3. How would you have felt if a curse was waiting for you if you didn't work your way to the other side?

Say, "Part of Shinto teaching insists you must do something to earn blessings in life. How would you have felt if the string was cut down and you were escorted to the other side and freely given the blessings?"

Ask, "How does this passage make you feel?" (Secure, happy, blessed, undeserving.) "According to these verses, how can we earn favor from God?" (We can't. God's favor is a gift from a gracious God.)

Then lead the class in a closing prayer like this one: "Father, we thank You for Your incredible grace. We know that we cannot earn Your favor by doing good works. We know You love us. You loved us so much that You gave Your Son for us. And You planned it all before the creation of the world. Thank You for all You give us and thank You for Your mercy. In Jesus' name we pray. Amen."

God blessed them and said to them, "Be fruitful and increase in number; fill the earth and subdue it. Rule over the fish of the sea and the birds of the air and over every living creature that moves on the ground." (Genesis 1:28 NIV)

Hear, O Israel: the LORD our God, the LORD is one. Love the LORD your God with all your heart and with all your soul and with all your strength. (Deuteronomy 6:4–5 NIV)

To whom, then, will you compare God?
What image will you compare Him to? (Isaiah 40:18 NIV)

The LORD is the everlasting God,
the Creator of the ends of the earth.
He will not grow tired or weary,
and His understanding no one can fathom. (Isaiah 40:28b NIV)

Then Jesus said to His disciples: "Therefore I tell you, do not worry about your life, what you will eat; or about your body, what you will wear. (Luke 12:22 NIV)

But seek His kingdom, and these things will be given to you as well. (Luke 12:31 NIV)

They exchanged the truth of God for a lie, and worshiped and served created things rather than the Creator—who is forever praised. Amen. (Romans 1:25 NIV)

He is the image of the invisible God, the firstborn over all creation. (Colossians 1:15 NIV)

All Scripture is God-breathed and is useful for teaching, rebuking, correcting and training in righteousness, so that the man of God may be thoroughly equipped for every good work. (2 Timothy 3:16–17 NIV)

There is no fear in love. But perfect love drives out fear, because fear has to do with punishment. The one who fears is not made perfect in love. (1 John 4:18 NIV)

Shinto—the National Worship of Japan

History

Shinto, the native religion of Japan, is one of the oldest religions in the world, combining ancient religious practices with such influences as Buddhism and Confucianism.

Central Teaching

Shinto is primarily a form of nature worship. Mountains, rivers, heavenly bodies, and other things are worshiped and personified (for example, Amaterasu, the sun spirit). This *animism* is based on the idea that the spirit *(anima)* is the seat of life. Everything has a spirit (a *kami*) and will act accordingly to its spirit. Human beings are not supreme rulers of the world, but members of the community with other beings—animals, plants, minerals, and the like. Rules, rituals, and worship help to maximize agricultural harvests and bring blessings to social units or territories while preventing destruction and ill fortune.

Significant People

Shinto has no real founder, no written scriptures, no body of religious law, and only a very loosely organized priesthood. Shinto is a nonexclusive religion, that is, people may practice Shinto along with a second or even third religion. Most Japanese practice Shinto and Buddhism.

Other Major Teachings

Practitioners of Shinto use four *affirmations* ("things we agree are good") to describe their basic beliefs:

1. Affirmation of the tradition and the family.
2. Affirmation of the love of nature.
3. Affirmation of physical cleanliness.
4. Affirmation of *matsuri* (festivals honoring the spirits).

The Shinto faith is expressed in all parts of life, such as architecture (*tori* gateways that mark the entrance to Shinto shrines are constructed out of wood with flowing water nearby for cleansing); art forms (*origami,* "paper of the spirits," dates from pre-writing days, when people took pieces of paper or fabric, whispered their prayers over them, and tied them on trees so that, when the wind blew, their prayers were repeated); and family life (worship of ancestors guarantees the solidarity of the family through reverential respect for one's father and for seniors in general, extending even to ancestors).

Prayers and sacrifices to ancestors can be offered at family altars where ancestors are visibly present in tablets. For important decisions and important occasions of one's life ancestors are consulted, that is, their graves are visited for reflection and meditation.

Contemporary Encounters

In North America there is a large and growing number of Japanese immigrants. They have imported their gardens with *tori* gates and other animistic features. Many of them will continue to hold Shinto beliefs even as they "try out" other religions.

Christian Connection

No human being is free from the temptation to idolatry, the worship of God's created things rather than the Creator Himself. We have this powerful message of Law to share with those of Shinto faith, along with the Good News that Jesus Christ has paid everything we owe, performed all the duties that are required, suffered, died, and rose from death so that we can be free from sin and have new life in Him.

The Way, the Truth, and the Life

When Mommy leaves for work, or a sibling heads off to school, or just about anyone heads out the door, a three-year-old will frequently ask, "Where are you going?" It's a natural question. And in many cases, the answer is very important to the child. No one likes to be left behind. As you read John 13:36–14:10, imagine what is going through the minds of the disciples. Then respond to these questions:

1. What prompted Peter's question to Jesus, "Where are You going?" (13:36)

2. Where was Jesus going? What steps would He take to get there? Why? Why are those important questions for us and all people?

3. What does Jesus mean when He tells Thomas, "I am the way and the truth and the life"? (14:6)

4. Why would a Shinto believer be amazed or troubled by Jesus' words?

5. The characteristics of God are revealed not only through the world He made, but through His Word and especially through His Son (14:7–8). What truths about God would you point out to those of Shinto faith?

Islam
Allah and His Prophet
Exodus 3:1–4:17

Study Outline: Islam

Activity	Time Suggested	Materials Needed
Opening Activities		
Begin with Prayer	2 minutes	
An Overview of Islam	10 minutes	Copies of Resource Page 6A; pencils
Studying the Word		
God Reveals Himself to Moses	15 minutes	Bibles
God Reveals Himself to Us	20 minutes	Bibles (and copies of the Apostles' Creed, if needed)
Applying the Word		
Jesus to Christians and Muslims	10 minutes	Bibles; Copies of Resource Page 6B; pencils
Closing Prayer	3 minutes	Hymnals or songbooks (optional)

Opening Activities

Begin with Prayer

Begin the class with prayer. You may use your own prayer, ask a class member to begin with prayer, or use the following prayer: "Heavenly Father, we thank You that Jesus was not only Your prophet, but also Your Son, and our Savior. We praise You for His death, because it gives us life. We praise You for His life, because it gives us a future and a hope. Help us trust what You have revealed to us about Yourself and help us understand the Islamic faith, that we may clearly witness to our faith to fellow Christians, Muslims, and people of no faith at all. Grant this to us, Father, because of Your Son, in whose name we pray. Amen."

An Overview of Islam

Provide the participants with copies of Resource Page 6A, "Islam— Allah and His Prophet," and pencils. You may either allow some quiet time so they can read the material on the resource page to themselves, or you may choose to have volunteers read aloud each section for the entire class. If the material is read aloud, you may wish to have another person write important words and phrases on the board or on newsprint as each section is read.

Additional points you might wish to add to the overview include:

- History—Islam, Judaism, and Christianity, are the world's three great *monotheistic* (only one God) faiths.

Objectives
The participants, through the study of God's Word and the power of the Holy Spirit, will

1. know the history and basic teachings of Islam;
2. be confident in God's love and mercy for all people, especially those who trust in His Son, Jesus Christ;
3. rejoice in and tell others of their heavenly Father's love.

- Central Teaching—The devoted Muslim will recite the *shahada (sha-HAY-da)* frequently.

- Significant People—Islam began more than 600 years after the birth of Christ (A.D. 610) and claims to "complete" God's revelation with a "final" prophet and "perfect" scriptures (see Revelation 22:18–19.)

- Major Teachings—Some also include the Jihad as one of the "pillars." *Jihad* means to strive or contend for the faith by any necessary means, including war (thus the general misconception that Jihad literally and only means "holy war"). Taken as a whole, the teachings of Islam are works-oriented and lacking in the concept of God's grace and mercy. Many Muslims are quite fatalistic ("as Allah wills").

- Contemporary Encounters—Islam has two main divisions or sects. *Sunnis* are the largest group (about 85 percent) and follow a more moderate interpretation of Islam. The *Shi'ites* are a more militant, conservative movement that dominates present-day Iran.

- Christian Connection—Islam misses out on the blessing of a saving relationship with a loving God who sacrificed His own Son out of steadfast mercy and enduring love.

Then ask the participants if they have any questions or need something clarified. Such questions may become the basis for continuing study by one or more volunteers from the class and reported back in a week or two.

Studying the Word

God Reveals Himself to Moses

Ask the class to name someone most of them know pretty well, perhaps a teacher or friend. Then ask what they know about this particular person *and how* such information is known. Most likely it is because the person has communicated information (revealed it) either directly by telling them, or by less direct means (for example, by loaning a magazine that has their address on it).

Remind the class that in the Bible we have information that God has directly revealed to us about Himself. Direct them to Exodus 3–4. Ask the class to scan the chapters. As they find information that God reveals about Himself, invite them to announce the verse and tell the information about God they find there. (They may point out some of the following: He is the God of Abraham, Isaac, and Jacob—3:6; He knows and cares about the suffering of His people and promises to deliver them—3:7-8; He reveals His name—3:13-15; He knows what will happen in the future—3:18-20; He is powerful—4:1-9; He is a God of promise, presence, and mercy—4:10-17.) Then discuss the following questions:

1. In what two ways has God revealed Himself reliably to us? (Through His written Word and through Jesus, the "Word made flesh." We also have limited knowledge of God through His creation.)

44

2. How is Jesus' revelation of God the Father greater than that of the prophets? (Point out Jesus' words in Matthew 9:6; John 1:18 and 34; John 8:19; and John 14:7-9—we can find out what God is like by knowing Jesus Christ.)

Conclude by saying the following:"An owner's manual for a video camera describes the camera's features and how it should be operated. In that same way, God tells us, in Jesus and in the Bible, who He is, what He does, and how much He loves us. How does this differ from Islam?" (Islam teaches that a believer can know God fully only through Muhammad—God's last and greatest prophet—and the Qur'an. We know that God came to us personally in His Son.)

God Reveals Himself to Us

God has revealed Himself to us through His Holy Word, through Jesus, and indeed through all that He has done. The Christian church has summarized what God has revealed in statements of faith called creeds (from the Latin word *credo* meaning "I believe"). The participants will most likely be familiar with the Apostles' Creed and the Nicene Creed. Each of these creeds is a statement of what the church knows and believes about God. The information contained in them is summarized from what God has told us in the Scriptures.

Ask volunteers to summarize in their own words what we say we believe about our God—Father, Son, and Holy Spirit—when we confess the creed. Then remind the class that Christians have always had creeds, from such basic statements as "Jesus is Lord" (Romans 10:9 and 1 Corinthians 12:3) to complex formulations like the Athanasian Creed.

Then ask volunteers to review the basic difference between the confession or witness of Muslims and that of Christians. (Muslims will confess that only Allah is the true God, and that Muhammad is his last and greatest prophet. Muslims also will stress living by the moral code known as "The Five Pillars of Islam." Christians will focus on the death and resurrection of Jesus Christ, believing that God forgives our sin and gives us the gift of salvation through faith in Jesus Christ.)

Applying the Word
Jesus to Christians and Muslims

Provide Bibles, pencils, and copies of Resource Page 6B, "What Do You Believe about Jesus?" to each participant. The resource page contains 14 teachings about Jesus that may be found either in the Bible or in the Qur'an. Give the participants time to circle items taught in the Bible (some biblical references are given to assist them) and to mark with an asterisk (*) items taught in the Qur'an.

After about five minutes, reveal the sources of the statements. (The Bible teaches all except B, M, and N; the Qur'an teaches A, B, C, D, E, F, G, and M. Neither the Bible nor the Qur'an teach that Jesus was married.) Then use the discussion questions to explore the implications of what they discover. Help them to recognize that the common beliefs

If your class is large, you may wish to do this activity in small groups. In small groups or as one group, it may be helpful to summarize the activity on newsprint or on the board.

If some in class are not familiar with the Apostles' or Nicene Creeds, have copies available for discussion. One or both can likely be found in your church's hymnal or worship book.

If You Have Time

Early Christians used an interesting way to confess their faith and identify themselves as believers that we still see today—the symbol of the fish. Ask each person to draw a simple fish figure on an index card. Then point out the following information: The Greek word for fish is ichthus (the same word from which we get our English word "ichthyology," meaning the study of fish). In Greek, ichthus is spelled

ΙΧΘΥΣ

This word is an acronym, a word formed from the first letters of the words in the Greek phrase

Ἰησοῦς Χριστὸς Θεοῦ Υἱός Σωτήρ

Encourage the participants to write both the Greek and

English phrases inside their fishes.

"Jesus Christ, Son of God, Savior" is an early Christian Creed. It revealed (that is, confessed) the Christian faith whenever a believer drew or displayed the fish. During times of persecution in the early church, it was used by Christians to share their faith secretly with one another. Ask volunteers to share ways that others may know we are Christians today.

between Christianity and Islam provide a starting place for dialog. Christians and Muslims (along with Jews) seem to acknowledge the same monotheistic God, though neither Jews nor Muslims have an understanding of His complete nature. Christians and Muslims can at least talk about Jesus as an important figure in their religions. In such a conversation a Christian might even have the opportunity to witness to what the Bible teaches about Jesus beyond what the Qur'an teaches. Beginning with some common ground, a Christian may hope for a better "hearing" of their witness. However, Christians should also understand that Muslims that convert to Christianity—or any other religion for that matter—are often shunned by their families and Islamic society in general. Therefore, Muslims do not find the Christian witness very attractive. Nevertheless, some common ground concerning Jesus exists between the two faiths.

Closing Prayer

Locate and share copies of the hymn "At the Name of Jesus" (found in many hymnals) as both a closing prayer and a confession of faith. Point out the theme of submission to God through faith in Jesus Christ that is present throughout the hymn. The participants may take turns praying/speaking the verses. The entire class may stand for verse 7 and read it in unison.

If you cannot find complete copies of the hymn, read the first and last stanzas below, or allow a volunteer to read them, as the closing prayer.

> At the name of Jesus Ev'ry knee shall bow,
> Ev'ry tongue confess Him King of glory now.
> 'Tis the Father's pleasure We should call Him Lord,
> Who from the beginning Was the mighty Word.
>
> Glory then to Jesus, Who, the Prince of light,
> To a world in darkness Brought the gift of sight;
> Praise to God the Father; In the Spirit's love
> Praise we all together Him who reigns above. Amen.

Resources

How to Respond: Muslims, Ernest Hahn, CPH, 1995

Muslim Friends, Roland E. Miller, CPH, 1995

Islam—Allah and His Prophet

History

In A.D. 610, a businessman named Muhammad (570-632), appalled by the worship of false gods in his hometown of Mecca in Saudi Arabia, began to preach submission to the one God Allah. He did this as a result of a vision of the angel Gabriel, who commanded him to bring God's message to the world and gave him the Qur'an, Islam's sacred scriptures. Today, Islam is the religion of about 20 percent of the world's population—second in number only to Christianity.

Central Teaching

The central confession in Islam is the *shahada*, "There is no God but Allah, and Muhammad is his prophet." *Muslim* means "one who submits." Islam teaches submission to God in all things. It is a code of honor, a system of law, and a way of life based on the Qur'an. The level of devotion to this moral code determines one's salvation.

Significant People

Muhammad, the founder of Islam, is considered Allah's last and greatest prophet. Muslims also believe that Abraham, Moses, and Jesus are great prophets. Jesus is not considered to be God's Son or the Messiah.

Other Major Teachings

Allah has sent prophets to his people. Adam was the first prophet, Muhammad the last. The Qur'an is Allah's only perfect and complete Word. Other scriptures—including the Jewish Torah, the Psalms, and the four Gospels—are acknowledged but not as perfect or complete. Muslims also believe in a spirit world, occupied by good angels and evil *jinn*.

To prepare for judgment, Muslims should live by a moral code that includes the Pillars of Islam: (1) Confession of faith—"there is no God but Allah, and Muhammad is his prophet." (2) Daily prayer according to a prescribed schedule and ritual. Muslims pray in the direction of the Sacred Mosque in Mecca, Islam's holiest city, called to prayer by cries of "Allahu akbar" (Allah is great). Muslims also worship at noon on Fridays. (3) Charity—All Muslims, except the very poor, are required to share two percent of their annual income with the poor. (4) Fasting at various prescribed times, especially during Ramadan, the holiest month of the Muslim year. (5) Pilgrimage—A pilgrimage to the city of Mecca, the birthplace of Muhammad, is expected of healthy and otherwise qualified Muslims at least once in a lifetime. This event draws well over two million pilgrims each year.

Contemporary Encounters

Islam is the world's fastest-growing religion and is found everywhere in the world and is growing in visibility in North America—espcially on college campuses and in large communities. A nineteenth-century heretical off-shoot, Baha'i, believes that another prophet, Baha'u'llah ("Glory of God"), was the last and greatest of God's prophets.

Christian Connection

The important Christian teaching to keep in mind when encountering Islam is that Jesus is not just a prophet: He is the Son of God, Savior of the world, and God's promised Messiah who died on the cross for the forgiveness of our sins.

What Do You Believe about Jesus?

What does the Holy Bible teach us about Jesus? First, circle each item in the list that is taught by Christianity. You can check your work using the Bible references given. Mark with an asterisk (*) each item that you think is taught in Islam.

A. Born of the Virgin Mary

B. A great prophet

C. Worked miracles

D. Taught the Gospel

E. Raised the dead

F. Ascended into heaven

G. Sinless

H. Son of God

I. Messiah

J. Savior of the world

K. Allowed by God to die on the cross

L. Resurrected from death

M. His mother was a prophet

N. Married

(Bible References: Mark 1:14–15; Luke 1:26–38; Mark 8:27–30; Mark 16:1–8; Luke 2:8–14; John 10:28–30; Hebrews 4:14–16; Luke 24:50–53; Luke 7:11–17; John 2:1–11; Matthew 21:10–11)

Questions for Discussion

• What common beliefs do Christians and Muslims share?

• How might a Christian find this common ground helpful?

Satanism and the Occult

Worshiping Evil

John 8:44; 2 Corinthians 4:4

Study Outline: Satanism

Activity	Time Suggested	Materials Needed
Opening Activities		
Prayer	5 minutes	
The Persuaders	10 minutes	Persuaders' speeches (on page 50)
Studying the Word		
An Overview	10 minutes	Copies of Resource Page 7A
Two Encounters with Satan	10 minutes	Bibles
Applying the Word		
Nine Satanic Sentences	15 minutes	Copies of Resource Page 7B, Bibles
Final Points to Remember about Satanism	5 minutes	Bibles
Closing Prayer	5 minutes	

Opening Activities

Prayer

Begin with a prayer like this one: "Heavenly Father, You are the God of truth, and You have revealed that truth to us through Your Word and through Jesus Christ. Send Your Holy Spirit among us now as we study the deception of Satanism and chase Satan away from us. Help us to resist him, so that we will not be easily fooled by his lies. Forgive us when we sin, bless us as Your children, and free us from the power of sin, death, and the devil through the work of Your Son, our Savior, Jesus. In His name we pray. Amen."

The Persuaders

Take two volunteers out of the room and appoint them Persuader 1 and Persuader 2. Give them copies of the boxed paragraphs and explain that Persuader 1 is a deceiver, and Persuader 2 always tells the truth. They are not to reveal their identities to the group, but they should try to present their points of view to the group as persuasively as possible.

Focus

Seeking to harness the power of evil is as old as religion itself. In all its forms, seeking rather than avoiding evil is both dangerous and offensive to our one true God. The most extreme form of this sinful behavior may be seen in the practice of satanism—the worship of Satan instead of God and the affirming in Satan's name of all that God warns us against.

Objectives

The participants, through the study of God's Word and the power of the Holy Spirit, will

1. recognize the reality and danger of Satan and his evil powers;

2. reject all forms of magic and divination that God condemns;

3. identify those trapped by satanism and show compassion to them through Jesus Christ;

4. rejoice in their place in God's kingdom through faith and His protection from all evil.

An Option

You may prefer to read the two statements from Persuader 1 and Persuader 2 yourself. Then let the group decide which one they would rather follow.

Persuader 1

You are very important to God. You are so important that He doesn't hold you accountable for your sins, but forgives every one of them. Since you are His children and He loves you so much, the most important thing to God is that you should be happy. He said we are no longer under the burden of the Law. So we should be able to do what we want to, right? He wants us to be happy, right? He forgives our sins, right? Why not do the things that make you happy? Live life the way you want to.

Persuader 2

God does love us and gave us Jesus to prove it. He does want us to be happy, but not with selfish indulgence. He wants us to be free in truth not from truth. He forgives us because Christ paid the price of sin on the cross. By our faith in Him, we are free from sin. The happiness God has for us is not a "feel good" happiness, but the joy that comes from truth. How can you indulge in sin and say you love God? You must choose one or the other.

Allow the two volunteers to *ad lib* further argument if they are able. Then have the class vote for the most persuasive of the two. Reveal the truth and falsehood perspectives of the persuaders and discuss their arguments. Ask these questions: "Did you guess who was telling the truth? How did you know? Or were you fooled? Why? Whose argument did you like better? Why?" Answers, of course, will vary.

Help the group analyze the statements. Point out that Persuader 1 used lots of truth among the lies, but didn't use the whole truth. This is one of Satan's favorite tricks. Persuader 1's argument breaks down when it contends that God wants us to be happy. This doesn't mean that God wants us to do anything that makes us *feel good*. God knows that real happiness is found in the forgiveness of sins and new life we have through Jesus Christ. Thus, Persuader 1 has lied and deceived.

Studying the Word
An Overview

Have the participants list ways that people feel powerful—their jobs, relationships, money, control, etc. Then ask, "Why do people seek these things? What do they do with the power they believe these things provide? What kind of things will people do to get or keep power? When are times you wish you had more control over others?" (Answers to these questions will vary according to the participants' experiences. Point out that for many people, power is not a positive tool but a negative weapon. The quest for power is a root cause for many who get involved in Satanism.)

According to *Webster's Encyclopedic Unabridged Dictionary of the English Language,* 1989, the definition seems simple:

> **Satanism**, n. (1) The worship of Satan or the powers of evil. (2) A travesty of Christian rites in which Satan is worshiped. (3) Diabolical or satanic disposition, behavior, or action.

Distribute copies of Resource Page 7A. Briefly review the six major points: (1) history, (2) central teaching, (3) significant people, (4) other major teachings, (5) contemporary encounters, and (6) Christian connection. You may wish to read aloud from the page or invite volunteers to read each section. After each section, invite questions and clarify the information. You may wish to assign some topics to participants for further study after the session.

Two Encounters with Satan

Divide the class into two groups. Assign one group to review Genesis 3 and the other to review Matthew 4:1–11. (If you have a large class, you might also assign Job 1:6–2:10.) As they review the Bible passages, write the following questions on the board or on newsprint for discussion. (Do not include the notes in parentheses; they are for use as you discuss the questions.)

1. Who does Satan challenge in these verses? (Genesis—Adam and Eve; Matthew—Jesus)

2. What is Satan's goal? (Satan always tries to turn people away from God.)

3. How does He approach his task? (In Genesis, he uses sophisticated logic and deception; in Matthew, he uses weakness and temptation.)

4. What are the results? (Adam and Eve disobey God and give in to Satan's wiles; Jesus, in His perfect obedience, resists Satan's temptations.)

5. What lessons can we learn in our own encounters with Satan? (Participants may mention the power of God's Word and the problem of Satan's lies. More detailed discussion points are provided below.)

After about five minutes, discuss the questions, allowing each group to respond according to the passage they explored.

To conclude this section make the following points: Satan has been attacking God's people since Adam and Eve were created. His tactics have not changed because human beings have not changed. Humans are still sinful and selfish. Satan uses our sinful nature to lure people away from God and into his domain. In fact, Satan uses the sin he committed to lure others into worshiping him. Satan wanted to be like God himself and was thrown out of heaven by God to roam the earth (Revelation 12:7–9). Satan knows that humans also want to be more like God, knowing the difference between good and evil, and having power over life. With this in mind, the devil has become an expert recruiter for turning God's people away from Him.

An Option

Instead of having the whole class study the Nine Satanic Sentences, you may break down into small groups and ask each group to evaluate one or two sentences and the activities that might go along with them. Have one person report to the rest of the group what their small group discussed.

Resources

How to Respond to the Occult, David W. Hoover, CPH, 1977

How to Respond to Satanism, Bruce G. Frederickson, CPH, 1988

Subtle Serpent, Darylann Whitemaarsh and Bill Reisman, Huntington House Publishers: Lafayette, Louisiana, 1993

www.religioustolerance. org/satanism.html

www.earthlight.co.nz/ users/spock/onaintro.html

cti.itc.virginia.edu/~jkh8x/soc 257/nrms/satanism/ churchof.html

Applying the Word

Nine Satanic Sentences

Distribute copies of Resource Page 7B and have the participants read the Nine Satanic Statements of Anton LaVey. Under each sentence, ask them to list the inappropriate activities that might be included in that sentence, and the godly actions God prompts in Christians through His Word and Spirit.

Also discuss these questions:

1. Why does Satanism continue to exist? (See 2 Corinthians 4:4 and John 8:44. As long as Satan exists, that is, until the final judgment, he will blind people to truth and deceive them about God's love.)

2. Why do people who worship Satan believe they are right?

   (Their minds are clouded. They believe what they want to believe, not the truth God reveals in His Word.)

3. Why can we trust God and not Satan? (There is no truth in Satan. He is a liar and deceiver and tells people what they want to hear. God's Word is the truth, and He is honest with everyone, even though this is, at times, much harder to hear than Satan's message.)

4. What is dangerous about Satan? (He is a deceiver; he can't be trusted. He makes people think they do not need a Savior.)

5. What is so great about God? (He tells the truth and gives us Jesus to rescue us from sin. His answer is the real thing.)

Final Points to Remember about Satanism

Conclude with these key points; you may wish to write them on the board or on newsprint as you speak or before class. If you have time, have individuals or everyone consult the Bible passages for the statements.

1. Satan is the father of all lies. (John 8:44)
2. Our struggle is against Satan. (Ephesians 6:12)
3. We are often deceived by Satan. (2 Corinthians 2:11)
4. Christ is victorious over Satan. (1 Corinthians 15:55–57)
5. Christ protects us from Satan's attacks. (Colossians 1:13–14)
6. Through Christ's strength, we can make Satan flee. (James 4:7)

Closing Prayer

Close with a prayer such as this one: "Dear Lord Jesus Christ, You defeated Satan when You took our sins upon Yourself and gave up Your life for us on the cross. You defeated his reign of power when You rose from the dead to conquer death for us. Please hold us in Your truth, Lord, so that we might not be so easily deceived by Satan. Keep us rooted in Your Word and guide our paths away from the evil one. Help us live lives that glorify You and find real joy in Your truth. In Your name we pray. Amen."

Satanism—Worshiping Evil

History

The term *satanism* is applied to many cults and movements, some of which pre-date the time of Christ and among which there is little unity. Even today, different satanic organizations vary in beliefs and practices.

Central Teaching

Traditional satanism emphasizes worship of a powerful, personal devil through cultic ritual and black magic. This form has not disappeared. Modern satanists frequently reject worship of Satan, but advocate instead that everyone indulge in whatever activity they want, without limit or restraint. This often includes satanic practices.

Significant People

Aleister Crowley (1875-1947) was an early leader of modern satanism in Great Britain. Raised in a Christian home, he became devoted to magic and the occult. Dissatisfied with existing occult organizations, Crowley started his own satanic group, the "Ordo Templi Orientis." He deplored Christian values and believed that evil would win the final battle over God.

Anton Szandor LaVey (1930-1997) was the force behind modern satanism. He felt Christianity was based on hypocrisy and that all religions elevated the spiritual—and denied the physical—aspects of humanity. In 1966 LaVey formed the Church of Satan. He wrote *The Satanic Bible* and *The Satanic Rituals*. Since his death, LaVey's daughter Karla has assumed leadership of the Church of Satan.

Other Major Teachings

The Church of Satan follows these guidelines for behavior:

- Prayer is useless; it distracts people from useful activity.
- Enjoy indulgence instead of abstinence. Practice with joy the seven deadly "sins" (greed, pride, envy, anger, gluttony, lust, and sloth).
- If someone smites you on one cheek, *smash* him on the other.
- Do unto others as they do unto you.
- Engage in sexual activity freely in accordance with your needs.
- Suicide is frowned upon.
- The satanist needs no elaborate, detailed list of rules of behavior.

(Adapted from information found at website *www.religioustolerance.org/satanism.html.*)

These beliefs appeal to sinful instincts and supports Satan's ends by telling sinners exactly what they want to hear.

Contemporary Encounters

Because satanism is frequently a do-it-yourself religion, it can spring up anywhere. Satanism as a religion is usually stumbled into by unsuspecting people, frequently teens, who are open to its lies for three primary reasons:

1. They are bored and seek excitement.
2. They are struggling with problems and are lured by easy solutions.
3. They seek power over others in black magic and secret rituals.

Christian Connection

The truth, especially the truth of God's Word, is a powerful weapon against Satan. Satanists themselves are being deceived (2 Corinthians 4:4). Christians can share the truth of Jesus Christ with Satan's followers, confident that the Holy Spirit will work through God's Word to defeat Satan in this world, even as he has ultimately been crushed through Christ's suffering, death, and resurrection.

Nine Satanic Sentences

The founder of the Church of Satan, Anton LaVey, has formulated *Nine Satanic Statements* that are summarized below. They represent the basic philosophy of modern satanism. But they are not God's plan for us. As you explore what the Bible says about each of these "satanic sentences," record ways you can reflect Christ's love in your life.

1. *Enjoy indulgence, not abstinence.* Look up Colossians 3:5–6.

2. *Live a vital existence, not spiritual pipe dreams.* Look up 2 Corinthians 5:7.

3. *Pursue undefiled wisdom, not hypocritical self-deceit.* Look up 1 Corinthians 2:4–5.

4. *Show kindness to those deserving of it, but waste no love on ingrates.* Look up Matthew 5:43–45a.

5. *Enjoy vengeance, not turning the other cheek.* Look up Romans 12:19–21.

6. *Give responsibility to the responsible; avoid concern for social parasites.* Look up Acts 20:35.

7. *Man is just another animal—the most vicious of all.* Look up Genesis 1:26–28.

8. *Seek gratification of all you desire.* Look up Romans 1:22–24 (or 22–32).

9. *Satan is the best friend the Christian church has had; he has kept it in business for centuries.* Look up the *real* friend of the Christian church in John 10:11–12.

Mormonism (Latter-day Saints)

"As God Is, Man May Become"
Galatians 1:6–9

Study Outline: Mormonism

Activity	Time Suggested	Materials Needed
Opening Activities		
Opening Prayer	5 minutes	
The Real Thing	10 minutes	3 varieties of dark soft drinks; 6-9 clear drinking glasses; masking tape
Check the Ingredients	10 minutes	Newsprint or marker board and markers
Studying the Word		
The Mormons	10 minutes	Copies of Resource Page 8A
No Other Gospel	15 minutes	Copies of Resource Page 8B; Bibles; prepared newsprint
Applying the Word		
Give It a Try	20 minutes	Bibles
Closing Prayer	5 minutes	

Opening Activities

Opening Prayer

Begin the session with a prayer like this one: "Dear heavenly Father, sometimes it is easy for us to believe in things that only appear to be real. At times something may look so good that we want to believe in it simply because it is outwardly appealing. Help us examine all spiritual things in the light of Your Word so that we may always find the truth. We ask for Your blessings on our time together. Help us be open and honest with each other, and help us see things through Your eyes. We ask this in Jesus' name. Amen."

The Real Thing

Before class prepare three sets of three clear glasses, filling one glass in each set, labeled #1, with a small quantity of Coke; fill three glasses with Pepsi, each labeled #2; and fill three glasses with root beer (or some other dark soda), each labeled #3.

When class is ready to begin, ask three people to help you with a taste test. Give them paper and pencils and require them to guess the identities of the soft drinks *without tasting them*. Then invite them to confirm their guesses by tasting the beverages.

Discuss the following questions, incorporating the suggested answers into discussion.

When the class is ready to begin, ask, "How can we identify which soft drink came from which container? Does it make a difference?"

1. How are the three sodas alike? (They are the same color, they are all bubbly.)

2. How are the three sodas different? (Different taste, different ingredients.)

3. Is there any way to positively identify them correctly? (Looks are deceiving; even taste can sometime be confusing. Scientific tests might be needed to identify their ingredients and match them to the manufacturers' formulas.)

Check the Ingredients

Point out that sometimes though things look alike—even though they may "taste" alike—when we check the ingredients we find they are not the same at all. In the same way, many religions have the appearance of Christianity, but when we look at them closely and check their ingredients we see that they are very different. That is the case with the religious group we will examine today: the Church of Jesus Christ of Latter-day Saints, often called Mormonism.

The Latter-day Saints are often described as a cult. Briefly discuss these points:

Most Cults …

1. **Deny some part of scriptural doctrine regarding Jesus.** (The cult may retain part of Jesus' background or aspects of who He is, but will deny what He has done to save us.)

2. **Have a leader with new revelation.** (Cults tend to center around a leader who claims to have new revelations that change, add to, or replace the authority of the Bible.)

3. **Have unique rituals and/or visible actions.** (These rituals or actions set the cult apart from the world: members often isolate themselves from society and in turn are viewed by society as isolated.)

4. **Redefine standard Christian terms.** (These groups may have new definitions for traditional terms that support their new ideas and give an appearance of orthodoxy to potential members.)

5. **Reject the early church.** (Cults frequently suggest that the church in its early years was corrupt and not the true church.)

6. **Are not consistent with either biblical doctrine or their own theology.** (Self-made religion is by nature flawed, prone to contradictions both within itself and with God's Holy Word.)

Studying the Word

The Mormons

Distribute copies of Resource Page 8A. Read aloud, or have volunteers read, the sections of this page, stopping briefly after each one to

Advance Preparation

This discussion may go more smoothly if you take time to write the heading and six main points (in bold print) on newsprint or on the board in advance. To avoid distraction, cover the board with newsprint, or lift the bottom edge of the printed newsprint to the top of the sheet and tape it in place, until this activity.

For Additional Study

Additional Bible verses that may be helpful in planning for this study are Genesis 2:7; Exodus 20:3; Deuteronomy 4:2, 6:4, 12:32, 18:14–22, 32:39; Psalm 89:6–8; Matthew 24:23–27; Luke 1:30–38; John 1:18; and Galatians 1:6–9.

answer questions or accept comments from the participants. Note that many questions may be more fully addressed on Resource Page 8B. There may be questions that you can't answer. Direct interested people to books on the resource list.

No Other Gospel

After explaining the aspects of a cult as defined previously, ask for a volunteer to read Galatians 1:6–9. Discuss the following questions:

1. What does St. Paul mean by "a different gospel"? (Something other than the truth taken directly from the Word of God as preached by Jesus Christ and His apostles. Point out that the Gospel of Christ has never changed. Preaching and teaching may use a variety of words, but the content remains the same.)

2. What concern in the Galatian congregation is Paul addressing? (They were new believers who were being drawn away from God's grace and pulled back to the Law. Some Jewish Christians from Judea were insisting that Gentile members of new churches needed to be circumcised and follow aspects of Jewish ceremonial law. In other words, the Gospel was not enough. Paul had similar concerns for the Corinthians [see 1 Corinthians 11:1–6].)

Explain that, just as the people in the early church tried to "make the Gospel better," so cults today insist that God's Word is not sufficient.

Distribute copies of Resource Page 8B, "No Other Gospel." Ask the class to look up the Bible verses related to each "truth," pick out the biblical truths from God's Word and write them in the proper space on the resource page. Allow approximately 10 minutes for this activity.

Then ask the question, "How do you think people can get involved in a group like this?" (It may look really good on the surface. Mormons are noted for taking care of each other, for being loyal to their families, for a low rate of juvenile delinquency, for being a caring, giving group, and for placing emphasis on education. Unfortunately, many people who are involved in this cult have no idea of what it is really all about. Much money is spent on advertising, particularly on television. On the surface everything looks great, including the wonderful pictures and statues of Jesus that are prominent throughout their temples.)

Applying the Word
Give It a Try

Remind the group that God wants all people to be saved. As God's people who know His saving truth, we have the privilege of sharing the Gospel with others—including people who are involved in cults such as the Mormons. Invite the participants to form pairs for a "Mormon-Christian" dialog. (You may need to be the partner for a leftover person.) Each person will have the opportunity to practice addressing the Gospel to, and listening to, a Mormon perspective. To get the dialogs going, try having the "Mormon" in each pair ask this question of the Christian: "Our congregation is offering a family night to introduce

To speed up this activity:

- Divide a large group into smaller groups of three to five people. (If your group is five or under, divide into groups of two and three.)
- Assign each group one or two of the Mormon truths. Have them assign one person in their group to write down what they discuss and one person to serve as a spokesperson for their group.
- Allow about five minutes for research and another minute or two for each group to report.

Resource List

For further information

How to Respond to the
Latter-day Saints, by Edgar P.
Kaiser, CPH 1977, 1995

Handbook of Today's
Religions, Josh McDowell and
Don Stewart, Thomas Nelson
Publishers, Nashville, 1983

people to our church. Would you like to come as my guest and learn more about the Church of Jesus Christ of Latter-day Saints?" Challenge the "Christian" to respond with a brief, warm, accurate statement of faith in Christ.

After each person has had an opportunity to assume both roles, brainstorm with the group the most helpful responses. Then share these helpful hints about witnessing to Mormons and others. If you have time, have volunteers look up the Bible verses for each guideline.

A. Speak with them in love. (1 Peter 3:15–17)

B. Share the Gospel and the love Jesus has shown in your own life. (Romans 1:16-17, 10:14-15)

C. Don't let them lead you astray. (1 John 2:24)

D. If you know the Scriptures *very* well and know Mormon teachings, you may be able to point out their errors and back up what you say with biblical information. However, do *not* try this approach unless you are sure you have the answers you need. Mormons have been well-taught to quote selected Scripture to emphasize their cause.

(Adapted from "Who's that Knocking at Your Door?" by Robert E. Smith, *Concordia Student Journal*, 1984).

Closing Prayer

Invite the group to join hands and pray for all people, especially Mormons. Invite participants, if they wish, to speak petitions when you pause in the middle of the prayer. Then pray:

"Dear Lord, we thank You for this time together. Thank You for allowing us to learn about other religions. Help us witness for You by what we do and who we are. Especially we pray for …"

Pause for others to pray. After everyone has had an opportunity to pray, close with the following:

"Help those we prayed for—even if we don't know who they are. We know that You want all people to be saved. Help us by Your Spirit to witness to Your love with our voices and our lives. We ask this in Jesus' name. Amen."

Mormonism—"As God Is, Man Can Become"

History

The Church of Jesus Christ of Latter-day Saints was begun by Joseph Smith, Jr., in 1830, in Fayette, New York. Smith claims to have translated the *Book of Mormon,* a primary source of their teachings, from golden "tablets" entrusted to him by the angel Moroni.

Smith took his new religion to a series of locations—Kirtland, Ohio, Independence and Far West, Missouri, and others. He finally founded his own community in Nauvoo, Illinois, where the church had its own laws and ordinances. Their unorthodox beliefs, especially polygamy, resulted in persecution. In 1844, Smith and his older brother were imprisoned for destroying an anti-Mormon publication. A mob attacked the prison and killed the brothers. Brigham Young became the new leader. To avoid further persecution, he moved the group to the Salt Lake valley where it flourished.

Central Teaching

Mormons believe that God was once a human being just like us and that we can become gods and earn admittance to a celestial heaven.

Significant People

In addition to Joseph Smith, Jr., (1805–1844) and Brigham Young, other important early leaders included Oliver Cowdery, who figured prominently in the founding, and Sidney Rigdon, an early convert and theologian in the Latter-day Saints who was passed over for leadership at Smith's death.

Other Major Teachings

Mormons do not believe in a triune God, but in three gods who are "united in love and purpose." There are three heavens and all people go to one of them. *The Celestial Kingdom* is the highest of the three.

To reach the celestial kingdom you must believe that Smith and his successors are true prophets, be baptized a Mormon, live a good life, obtain a celestial marriage, bear many children, attend all church functions, and pay tithes to the church. Mormons may not drink alcohol or hot beverages. They must not use tobacco and must observe many other strict practices.

Mormon doctrine includes *progressive revelation*—the most recent revelations of the current living prophet supersede previous doctrines in their authoritative writings, so their doctrines change. Though it was once accepted, the Latter-day Saints no longer condone polygamy. Similarly, African-Americans could not achieve celestial heaven until a new revelation in 1978.

Contemporary Encounters

The highest concentration of Mormons is in Utah and the Hawaiian islands. Tabernacles have been erected in all parts of the United States and are under construction or planned for all major continents. Christians will encounter them in the workplace, in schools, and in every avenue of life. To the average person, this group appears to be very Christian. Mormon membership has grown to more than 8.3 million members worldwide, 4.5 million in the United States.

Christian Connection

Christians believe in one triune God through whom we have salvation by God's grace alone, not by our efforts. The Bible is God's unchanging truth and our only authority for teaching. The *Book of Mormon,* on the other hand, has seen over 3,000 changes since it was first written.

No Other Gospel

Mormon	Scripture	Christian
1. Progressive Revelation—The "living prophet" (head of the church) of the Mormon Church may have revelations. The most recent revelation takes precedence over all past revelations and is considered true even if it contradicts a past revelation.	Matthew 5:17–19	1. Unchangeable Authority of God
2. Many Sources of Belief—Based on four books: *Doctrines and Covenants*, *The Pearl of Great Price*, *The Book of Mormon*, and *The King James Version of the Bible*, to the extent that it is interpreted correctly.	Revelation 22:18–19	2. The Bible
3. God Was Once a Man Like We Are—Jesus, like God before Him, was born of His Father. Later he was reborn through a man and a woman. Through obedience, He earned way to the celestial kingdom and godhood, taking His wives with Him.	Numbers 23:19, Psalm 90:2, Acts 12:21–23	3. God as Supreme Being
4. We Can Become Gods—Just like God before us, we can do this through good works. If you do well, you are placed in celestial heaven and can work your way up to godhood.	Genesis 3:1–6, 22–24	4. There Is Only One God
5. Three Heavens—*Celestial* heaven is for those Mormons who do enough good works on earth. *Terrestrial* heaven is for those who don't do well or are honorable non-Mormons. *Telestial* heaven is for those who are wicked.	Ephesians 2:8–10, John 17:24–25	5. Saved by Grace.

One God, Many Gods **Resource Page 8B** © 1998 CPH

Jehovah's Witnesses

Jehovah Who?

Isaiah 43:10 and Philippians 2:9

Study Outline: Jehovah's Witnesses

Activity	Time Suggested	Materials Needed
Opening Activities		
Opening Prayer	5 minutes	
We Know God	10 minutes	Bibles
Do They Know God?	15 minutes	Copies of Resource Page 9A
Studying the Word		
A Response from God's Word	20 minutes	Copies of Resource Page 9B; Bibles
Applying the Word		
Encountering Jehovah's Witnesses	10 minutes	Newsprint or marker board and markers (optional)
Closing Prayer	5 minutes	

Opening Activities

Opening Prayer

Being with a prayer like this one: "Dearest Jesus, You came to earth as both true God and true man to pay for the sins of all people. There is no other way to heaven except through You. As we study the Jehovah's Witnesses, give us words that will help us to tell others about salvation through You. We ask it in Your name. Amen."

We Know God

Begin by asking the question, "Who is God?" Invite responses from several volunteers. Probe for a response that includes God as Father, Son, and Holy Spirit. Then ask, "How do you *know* who God is?" (God gives us faith to believe what He teaches in the Bible.) Then ask, "Do you believe everything the Bible says?" (They will likely answer yes. If they don't, remind them that the whole Bible is God's revealed Word.) Then point out that some groups add, take away from, or misuse the message of the Bible to divert attention from Jesus and His free gift of salvation. Mention that today's lesson will focus on the teachings of the Jehovah's Witnesses.

Do They Know God?

Distribute copies of Resource Page 9A. Invite volunteers to read it aloud. After each section invite questions or comments by the class. Incorporate the following comments into discussion.

Focus

Jehovah's Witnesses, originally known as The Watchtower Bible and Tract Society, spread their beliefs through their own version of the Bible and other Watchtower publications. They believe in a one-person God whom they know as Jehovah, but they deny that Jesus Christ and the Holy Spirit are God and seek eternal life through obedience and dedication. Our triune God—the real Jehovah—offers eternal life as a free gift to all who believe through the power of the Holy Spirit in the perfect life and sacrificial death of Jesus Christ, true God and God's Son.

Objectives

The participants, through the study of God's Word and the power of the Holy Spirit, will

1. compare the beliefs of the Jehovah's Witnesses to those of the Bible;
2. grow in faith in the triune God;
3. give thanks for God's free gift of salvation through faith.

An Option

If you or someone in your class has had a recent visit from a Jehovah's Witness, stage a roleplay of a conversation that might take place at someone's door.

Let the person with experience portray the Witness to recreate what might happen during such a visit.

If You Have Extra Time

Ask, "Where does the name Jehovah come from?" (This name for God never appears in the Bible. Zealous Jews took the consonants of God's name in Hebrew, "Yahweh," and the vowels from the Hebrew word for "Lord" and created the word <u>Jehovah</u> by which they could identify God without misusing His personal name by speaking it aloud. The Jehovah's Witnesses believe that Jehovah is the only real name for God, and yet, the name does not even appear in God's Word. They hold confidently to this false assertion because, to them, the Bible only reveals part of God's truth. They believe that those who write their publications, <u>The Watchtower</u> and others, know the <u>whole</u> truth.

To save time, or to make this activity easier for classes with limited Bible study skills, assign each of the seven statements to a different individual, pair, or small group. After allowing a few minutes for their work on that one statement, allow them to report in turn on the statements.

History: Russell began as the "pastor" of a small Bible study group in Pittsburgh at the age of 18 with no formal theological training. From that small beginning, a world-wide organization has blossomed with very unorthodox views.

Central Teaching: God created mankind and gave Satan temporary dominion over the earth in order to prove that His human creations could remain faithful and obedient to Him. According to the Witnesses, Jesus—who is not God, but just a spiritual being (the archangel Michael) before and after He was on earth and only a human being while on earth—began His second coming and Jehovah's everlasting kingdom on earth in 1914. As a result of His second coming, Satan's dominion will soon be destroyed and God's government will be established.

Significant People: Faithful Jehovah's Witnesses do not question the teachings of the leaders who guide the church and publish its magazines. This small core has incredible power.

Other Major Teachings:

- "Hell" is not a spiritual existence after death, but merely the end of existence for those who are not "saved."
- Salvation is purely a matter of obedience and good works in the view of the Jehovah's Witnesses.

Contemporary Encounter: If any participants have had recent contact with Jehovah's Witnesses, invite them to share their experiences.

Christian Connection: Stress the nonbiblical teachings of the Jehovah's witnesses that divert attention from Jesus and His free gift of salvation. Comment that when we have opportunity to talk with them, we can share the confidence we have in God's grace and the source of our faith—the Bible's message of the Gospel.

There may be questions raised that you cannot answer. You may wish to refer interested participants to the list for resource for further study later in this chapter.

Studying the Word
A Response from God's Word

Distribute copies of Resource Page 9B. Direct the participants to look up the Bible passages after each statement of Jehovah's Witnesses beliefs and make notes about what the Bible says in each case.

After allowing about 10 minutes for their work, share the following comments about the Jehovah's Witnesses' beliefs and invite volunteers to suggest scriptural responses.

1. Jehovah's Witnesses teach that *Jehovah* is the only name for God. But Jesus says in John 10:30, "I and the Father are one," and God Himself has given His Son the name of Jesus. How can the name of Jesus (Philippians 2:9) be above every name—including Jehovah—if Jehovah is the only *real* name? The Bible uses many names for the triune God.

2. Jehovah's Witnesses teach that Christ sacrificed only a human body, since He was not God nor, while here on earth, even a spiritual being. However, Colossians 2:9 teaches, "For in Christ all the fullness of the Deity lives in bodily form," and 1 Peter 2:24 teaches, "He Himself bore our sins in His body on the tree." Jesus made a divine-human sacrifice, not a simple human sacrifice.

3. The Jehovah's Witnesses teach that the perfect man, Adam, fell into sin, condemning all His offspring. Therefore, God sent Jesus to sacrifice His human body for Adam's human body. However, Romans 6:10 says, "The death He died, He died to sin once *for all*" (emphasis added).

4. The Jehovah's Witnesses teach that you must prove your worthiness of salvation. They also teach that the work of Jesus is not finished, so there is no security in their salvation. They merely *hope* to have the chance to prove to God that they deserve heaven. The Bible teaches that those who believe in Jesus Christ have been given eternal life already (John 3:36, John 5:24, and 1 John 5:13). Our salvation is complete, and we need never doubt it.

5. Jehovah's Witnesses teach that faith in Christ's sacrifice alone is not enough to merit heaven. You must do good works such as studying and reading the *Watchtower* (a magazine put out by the Jehovah's Witnesses), making door-to-door calls, and attending meetings. The Bible clearly teaches that good works do not bring us salvation (Ephesians 2:8–9, Romans 3:24, and 1 John 1:7).

6. The Jehovah's Witnesses forbid prayer to Jesus. They teach that those who do so could lose even the possibility of salvation. The Bible teaches in 1 John 2:22–23, "Who is the liar? It is the man who denies that Jesus is the Christ. Such a man is the antichrist—he denies the Father and the Son. No one who denies the Son has the Father; whoever acknowledges the Son has the Father also."

7. *The Watchtower* restricts heaven to 144,000 people according to Revelation 14:1–3, and relegates all others to eternity on earth. They ignore all other clear Scripture passages that teach salvation for all who believe, but damnation for those who do not believe. Romans 3:22–24 says, "This righteousness from God comes through faith in Jesus Christ to all who believe. There is no difference, for all have sinned and fall short of the glory of God, and are justified freely by His grace through the redemption that came by Christ Jesus." See also Mark 16:16.

Applying the Word
Encountering Jehovah's Witnesses

God's Word urges us to testify to the truth as witnesses to Jesus. While faith discussions at our doorstep may make us uncomfortable, such conversations could well be the means the Holy Spirit uses to redirect the faulty beliefs of those whom God also loves.

Share the following simple suggestions with the class to help them stay focused and give a clear witness of their faith. If possible, write these guidelines on the board or on newsprint or prepare copies for each participant to have.

An Option

You can have a student role-play what might happen if a J. W. came to your door. You could also use the conversation written out in the 1977 CPH booklet, How To Respond to Jehovah's Witnesses, pages 19–21. This booklet is excellent background reading.

For Further Study

How to Respond to Jehovah's Witnesses, Herbert Kern, CPH, 1977, 1995

The Religious Bodies of America, F. E. Mayer, CPH, 1961

Handbook of Denominations in the United States, Frank Mead, revised by Samuel Hill, new ninth edition, Abingdon Press, 1985, Nashville

Churches in America, Thomas Manteufel, CPH, 1994

1. When you encounter the Jehovah's Witnesses (probably at your door) be friendly and tell them that you are *a believer in Jesus.* (Remember they see Christian churches as part of Satan's kingdom.)

2. Pray to the Spirit for help when you realize you must testify to the Witnesses.

3. Jehovah's Witnesses are not accustomed to a loving message and free salvation. Remember, they are trying to earn heaven. After you listen to them, tell them that you have peace knowing that if you were to die tonight, you would live forever with Jesus.

4. Your witness could include these points:

   a. You trust in Jesus and His Word, not an organization. God's free gift is yours solely by grace through faith in Jesus (John 3:16).

   b. You know eternal life is yours (1 John 5:13, John 14:1-6).

   c. You are not saved by what you do, but you do good works out of love for God (Ephesians 2:8-10).

   d. Ask for their name so that you can pray for them by name. Tell them you are going to pray that they too may know peace through Jesus.

(Adapted from *How to Respond to Jehovah's Witnesses,* Herbert Kern, CPH, 1977, 1995.)

Remind your students that most Jehovah's Witnesses are well trained to refute those who witness to them about the Good News. The point is not to "win arguments" but to plant "Gospel seeds." If you have time, allow volunteers to practice the outline with you in a roleplay, or let the whole class pair up for practice. Remind them that God will work through their words by the power of His Holy Spirit to accomplish His will—the success of their testimony is not based on their efforts.

Closing Prayer

Conclude the session with a prayer for the salvation of all those God loves, including Jehovah's Witnesses. You may wish to use this prayer: "Dear God, You are the Father, the Son, and the Holy Spirit. Teach us how to witness to the Jehovah's Witnesses so that they may be rescued from their sins, just as we also have been rescued from ours through Jesus Christ, our Lord. Give us the words to speak and the compassion to overcome their false teachings with Your Word and Your Spirit. Thank You for the wonderful free gift of our salvation through Jesus and forgive us when we take that gift for granted. Help us be prepared to testify to You at all times. In Jesus' name we pray. Amen."

Jehovah's Witnesses—Jehovah Who?

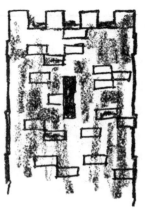

History

Charles T. Russell (1852–1916) founded *The Watchtower Bible and Tract Society* in Pennsylvania in 1872. In 1879, he published *Zion's Watchtower* in which he detailed his own unique interpretations of Scripture. The group became officially known as Jehovah's Witnesses in 1931, though it had been informally known that way since 1914. Now the Witnesses claim world-wide membership of over 5.5 million with over 20 percent of them in the United States.

Central Teaching

Jehovah's Witnesses believe that they have been organized to announce the early establishment of God's rule on earth.

Significant People

Charles T. Russell was the founder and author of most of the *Studies in the Scriptures* that outline the group's teachings. His successor, Joseph F. Rutherford, moved the organization to Brooklyn, New York, and established the governing body, a small group of men who continue to direct the work and determine the teachings of the Witnesses.

Other Major Teachings

The Witnesses use *The Watchtower,* first published in 1879, to interpret the Bible and as their main means for spreading their doctrine. They also have their own version of the Bible called the *New World Translation.*

Jehovah's Witnesses believe that Adam was created to be perfect, but when he sinned, he lost the right of eternal life for all of his offspring, that is the whole world. Jesus Christ, who is the "created" Son of God (but not Jehovah Himself), was sent to earth to be a perfect and blameless human to pay for Adam's sin. This opens the door for us to prove our worthiness. The Witnesses deny hell and claim that only 144,000 will be in heaven while the rest of the faithful will be on the new earth. They also believe that they are called to gather the other "sheep" thus earning their place on the new earth.

Contemporary Encounters

It seems likely that most everyone will encounter Jehovah's Witnesses at their own doorstep at some time or another. Door-to-door witnessing is the only activity of members on which records are kept and is the most important requirement for their salvation.

Christian Connection

Christians can hold fast to three basic teachings of Scripture in their witness to the Witnesses: (1) God's Word in the Bible is the only source for all our knowledge about God and His plan for salvation; (2) salvation is not earned by good works, but is ours by God's grace through faith in Jesus Christ; and (3) Jesus Christ is shown in the Bible to be true God and God's Son, and it is through His suffering, death, and resurrection that *all who believe* have forgiveness for sin and eternal life with God in heaven.

A Response from God's Word

Jehovah's Witnesses	Christianity
1. The only proper name for God is *Jehovah*.	John 10:30; Philippians 2:9
2. Christ sacrificed a mere human body.	Colossians 2:9; 1 Peter 2:24
3. Christ gave His life as a ransom for Adam only.	Romans 6:10
4. Salvation is only a future possibility not a present reality, because neither our work nor Christ's is yet done.	John 3:36; John 5:24; 1 John 5:13
5. Faith in Christ is not enough for our salvation; we must merit heaven through our obedience.	Ephesians 2:8–9; Romans 3:24; 1 John 1:7
6. Since Jesus is not God, praying to Him is unthinkable idolatry.	1 John 2:22–23
7. Only 144,000 will enter heaven. All others will dwell on the "new earth" eternally.	Romans 6:10; Romans 3:22–24

One God, Many Gods   **Resource Page 9B**

Scientology
A Theology of Mental Health
2 Timothy 1:9–10

Study Outline: Scientology

Activity	Time Suggested	Materials Needed
Opening Activities		
Opening Prayer	3 minutes	
Too Good to Be True	10 minutes	
Studying the Word		
A Sketch of Scientology	10 minutes	Copies of Resource Page 10A
Finding the Answers	20 minutes	Copies of Resource Page 10B, pencils, Bibles
Applying the Word		
Filling the Void	10 minutes	Copies of Resource Page 10B
Praying for the Empty	5 minutes	

Opening Activities

Opening Prayer

Begin with a prayer like this one: "Heavenly Father, to those who don't know You, Your promises may seem too good to be true. Today as we look at some of the empty promises of false religion, give us a renewed joy in knowing the truth of Your promises. We especially praise You for the promise fulfilled in the coming of Your Son, Jesus Christ, to save our world from sin. Make us witnesses of this Good News to all those whose hearts long for a promise that is true. In Jesus' name we pray. Amen."

Too Good to Be True

Ask a volunteer to explain the meaning of the phrase "Too good to be true." Point out that we all know the saying, "If something sounds too good to be true, it probably is." Ask the participants to give examples of advertisements they have seen or heard that seem too good to be true. (Examples may include get-rich-quick schemes, miracle diets or exercise machines, beauty creams, free vacations, sweepstakes mailings, and the like.) If friendly competition motivates your group, divide them into teams and reward the group that comes up with the longest list of specific "too good to be true" advertisements.

Ask what is appealing about these advertisements, using some of their specific examples. If you are comfortable doing so, you might share a time when you fell for something that turned out too good to be true. Others in the group might be willing to do the same.

Focus

With a vocabulary all their own, the followers of L. Ron Hubbard seek salvation by "clearing themselves of engrams," becoming free of their cycle of reincarnation, and enjoying immortality as "operating thetans" (thay-tns). They profess no need of a God who loves them, who died for their redemption in the person of Jesus Christ, and who lives in those who have faith in Christ through the Holy Spirit's power.

Objectives

The participants, through the study of God's Word and the power of the Holy Spirit, will

1. identify the many conflicts between Scientology and God's Word;
2. be strengthened in their faith in the triune God who loves them;
3. learn to share their Christian faith in a winsome way.

An Option

If your group has dramatic talent, divide them into groups and challenge them to ad lib an advertisement that is too good to be true. Or call on several volunteers ahead of time to create a brief advertisement for Scientology, using the promises presented in this lesson.

Another option is to bring in a few magazines or

tabloid newspapers and invite the class to find ads that are too good to be true.

If you have internet access, you can find more information about Scientology and its founder at www.scientology.org or www.lronhubbard.org

An Option

If your group is large, divide them into smaller groups and assign each one or two questions on the chart to research. Have them write their findings on large sheets of newsprint or poster board to report back to the class.

If your group has lots of Bible knowledge, challenge them to come up with additional Bible verses or accounts that answer the questions on the chart.

(The information in the Scientology column of the chart was taken from What is Scientology? (Los Angeles: Bridge Publications, 1992), a slick and colorful 833-page advertisement for the Church of Scientology printed under the guise of a "Comprehensive Reference on the World's Fastest Growing Religion." If a copy is available at your local library, it would be an excellent visual of Scientology's skill at making an appealing presentation.)

Say, "Today we will be looking at a religion that promises a way to solve all your problems, accomplish all your goals, achieve lasting happiness, and even gain immortality. It sounds too good to be true, but a lot of people believe that it is. The religion we will be looking at today is Scientology."

Studying the Word
A Sketch of Scientology

Explain to the group that Scientology is a relatively new religion founded by a man named L. Ron Hubbard in 1954. Hubbard also had a career as a novelist, and many of the terms that Scientologists use sound like something out of a science fiction novel. Distribute copies of Resource Page 10A and direct the participants' attention to the Central Teaching and the Other Major Teachings. This will give the group a brief overview of the Church of Scientology.

Finding the Answers

Distribute copies of Resource Page 10B. Read the opening paragraph under "Finding the Answers" aloud to the group. Then work through the chart, using the Bible references to form a Christian response to each question. Encourage the participants to fill in the chart as you go.

Use the information that follows to inform discussion of each of the questions on the chart.

1. **Is human nature good or evil?** Psalm 51:5—We were all born sinful. Romans 3:12—We have all turned away from God, and no one can claim to be good.

2. **What is truth?** John 8:31-32—God's Word is truth. John 14:6—Jesus Himself is the truth.

3. **What is the root of our problems?** Genesis 3:16-19—All of our problems originate in the Garden of Eden, when Adam and Eve fell into sin and received God's judgment. Romans 5:12—When sin entered the world, the curse of death came with it. Galatians 6:7-8—When we live to please our sinful nature, trouble follows.

4. **What is the answer to our problems?** John 16:33—Jesus encourages us saying that even though we have troubles in this world, He has overcome this world. Acts 4:12—The *only* way of salvation is through Jesus Christ. Romans 8:31, 35, 37-39—God is on our side, and *nothing* can separate us from His love. 1 Peter 5:7—God encourages us to give our troubles to Him, because He cares for us.

5. **Who is Jesus?** Matthew 1:21—Jesus was promised to be the one to save all people from sin. Matthew 16:15-16—Peter professes that Jesus is "the Christ, the Son of the living God." Mark 1:9-11—At Jesus' baptism, God declares Him to be His Son. John 11:25-26—Jesus calls Himself "the resurrection and the life," the One who has power over death.

6. **Is there eternal life?** John 3:16—God clearly promises eternal life to all who believe in His Son, Jesus Christ. John 10:27–28—Jesus, our Good Shepherd, promises to give eternal life to His sheep.

Once the chart is completed, it may be helpful to invite volunteers to give a brief verbal summary of what the group has found.

Applying the Word

Filling the Void

Say to the group, "Even with its bizarre concepts and vocabulary, the Church of Scientology attracts a lot of devoted followers. They include, as we have seen, celebrities we know well, such as John Travolta and Tom Cruise. What do you think attracts these people to Scientology?" (Answers may include its promises of a happy, problem-free life, the chance to earn immortality.) Explain to the group that Scientology is particularly attractive to people experiencing emptiness in their lives. People who are lonely or burdened by some kind of trouble are anxious for answers and vulnerable to the claims of Scientology. Just as a balding man might believe in a hair-growing cream or a fatigued mother of small children might buy "super-energy pills," empty people seek happiness in the claims of Scientology.

Possibly the greatest appeal of Scientology is that it is something you can *do for yourself*. If you pay the money and take the courses, Scientology promises to teach you methods to unlock the hidden potential within yourself. Scientology promises you control of your own life, which is very appealing in a world that often seems out of control. Discuss the following questions:

1. Relying on yourself to overcome your problems, achieve happiness, and find eternal life sounds appealing, but what is the downside of this? (The downside, of course, is that we are not capable of doing this on our own. Relying on ourselves only sets us up for failure and despair.)

2. What does the Bible have to say about relying on ourselves for help and salvation? (Praise God, we don't have to. Salvation is a gift of God that does not depend on our effort.) Direct attention to the Bible passage printed in the last section of Resource Page 10A. Ask for a volunteer to read the passage aloud while the group follows along. Say to the group, "This passage is a wonderful reminder that we don't need to rely on ourselves for help and salvation. Even before time began, God gave us His grace and salvation. This is one promise that may sound too good to be true, but we know that it is certainly true."

Remind the the participants that not everyone lives with the joy of this good news. Ask them to think about some of the empty people who might be vulnerable to the claims of Scientology. Ask volunteers to share what kind of Christian witness they might give to a person who is (1) lonely, (2) grieving a loss, (3) feeling dissatisfied with life, (4) having problems in relationships, or (5) afraid of death. Challenge them to use what they have learned in today's lesson in their responses.

An Option

If your group has drama talent, invite volunteers to role-play their responses to the people experiencing emptiness.

69

Closing Prayer

Use the closing prayer time to make this lesson more personal for the participants. Before the closing prayer, ask them to think of someone they know personally who is feeling empty or troubled for some reason. It could be someone who has experienced the loss of a loved one, someone who is ill, or anyone who is experiencing any kind of difficulty. Explain that they will be lifting up this person in silent prayer as part of today's closing. When everyone has had the opportunity to think of an individual, close with this prayer:

"Lord, so many people in our world are looking for happiness and salvation. We thank You, Lord, that we belong to You, and that we know Your awesome love for us and Your promise of salvation. Today we pray for all those people who are struggling in any way. We pray that they would not be taken in by empty promises that are too good to be true. We pray that they would not rely on themselves and find despair, but turn to You and find hope. Lord, we especially pray for these people that we silently mention in our hearts. (Observe a time of silence.) Be with them whatever their needs are and use us to speak Your Good News to them. In Jesus' name we pray. Amen."

Scientology—a Theology of Mental Health

History

Scientology was founded in 1954 by L. Ron Hubbard. The movement began with the popularity of Hubbard's book, *Dianetics: The Modern Science of Mental Health*.

Central Teaching

Using the methods of Scientology, people are capable of raising their own spiritual awareness to the point of achieving immortality. Those who reach this level are called "Operating Thetans" (thay-tns).

Significant People

Scientology is based solely on the many writings of L. Ron Hubbard. Among the members of the Church of Scientology are numerous celebrities, including John Travolta, Tom Cruise, Kirstie Alley, and Lisa Marie Presley.

Other Major Teachings

Students of Scientology, called "preclears," are first taught a method called "auditing" that is designed to clear their mind of "engrams" (negative mental images). Once students reach a state of "clear," they follow the steps on the "bridge to total freedom" with the goal of becoming "operating thetans."

Operating thetans are said to have "complete spiritual freedom," including immortality.

Contemporary Encounters

L. Ron Hubbard's writings are widely available in bookstores or other places where books are sold. *Dianetics*, his most famous title, is widely marketed as a self-help book. Possibly the greatest exposure for the Church of Scientology comes through the endorsement of its celebrity members, who donate money and make appearances on behalf of the church.

Christian Connection

Scientology calls on individuals to tap their own powers to overcome the problems of life and eventually achieve eternal life. Thanks be to God that, as Christians, we do not have to rely on ourselves for salvation! In our Baptism, we are claimed by a God "who has saved us and called us to a holy life—not because of anything we have done but because of His own purpose and grace. This grace was given us in Christ Jesus before the beginning of time, but it has now been revealed through the appearing of our Savior, Christ Jesus, who has destroyed death and has brought life and immortality to light through the Gospel." (2 Timothy 1:9–10)

Scripture quotation: NIV®. Used by persmission of Zondervan.

One God, Many Gods

Finding the Answers

Scientology offers its own answers to some of the basic questions of life. Below are some teachings of the Church of Scientology. Using the Bible, write Christianity's answers to these same questions.

	Scientology	Christianity
1. Is human nature good or evil?	People are basically good, not evil.	Psalm 51:5; Romans 3:12
2. What is truth?	What each person finds to be true for himself is true.	John 8:31–32; 14:6
3. What is the root of our problems?	Problems, illness, and unhappiness come from a lack of awareness of ourselves and our surroundings.	Genesis 3:16–19; Romans 5:12; Galatians 6:7–8
4. What is the answer to our problems?	Scientology teaches methods to free minds of "engrams" (negative mental images) to become "clear." The goal is to become an "operating thetan" with "complete spiritual freedom" who rises above all problems.	John 16:33; Acts 4:12; Romans 8:31, 35, 37–39; 1 Peter 5:7
5. Who is Jesus?	Although the cross is a part of the Scientology logo, Jesus is rarely mentioned in their teachings. His death symbolizes the triumph of the spirit over the body.	Matthew 1:21; 16:15–16; Mark 1:9–11; John 11:25
6. Is there eternal life?	"Operating thetans" are free from the cycle of birth and death. They become immortal.	John 3:16; 10:27–28

One God, Many Gods   **Resource Page 10B**   © 1998 CPH

New Age Thinking

Everyone and Everything Is God?

1 John 2:20–25, 28

Study Outline: New Age Thinking

Activity	Time Suggested	Materials Needed
Opening Activities		
What's New?	10 minutes	Bibles; newsprint and markers
A Look at the New Age	15 minutes	Copies of Resource Page 11A
Studying the Word		
Sound Good?	10 minutes	Copies of Resource Page 11B; Bibles
Applying the Word		
What Now?	15 minutes	Continued on Resource Page 11B
Closing Prayer	5 minutes	

Opening Activities

What's New?

Invite the participants to help you create a list of fashions, activities, toys, or music that might once have been considered "old-fashioned," but have recently made a come-back. List their suggestions on newsprint or on the board. (Specific items will vary regionally, but might include roller skates/in-line skates and sheath dresses.) Point out that often what seems new is really something old that has been recycled. New trends we believe will last quickly disappear, only to surface later. Each generation believes they are unique, with their own ideas, preferences, and problems. Yet, God reminds us that "there is nothing new under the sun" (Ecclesiastes 1:9).

Ask the class to list ways in which people have *not* changed over the years. (People have always been concerned about their appearance, afraid of the unknown, and jealous of others.) Conclude by saying, "God sent us Jesus—as Savior and friend—because He knew we would always be wrestling with a very old problem: our sinful nature. Today we're going to take a look at a religious philosophy that offers a *new* way of handling the *old* problem of sin. It's called the New Age Movement. But there's nothing really *new* about it."

Invite the participants to join you in this prayer: "Father, thank You for being a tried-and-true God whom we can depend on in all our struggles. Help us examine all things, old and new, with Your wisdom and truth. May the light of our Savior, Jesus Christ, continue to shine into the dark and confusing areas of our lives. We ask it in His name. Amen."

Focus

The New Age Movement uses crystals, channeling, meditation, and all kinds of mystic arts to find salvation—oneness with God—in self-awareness and psychic healing. Their beliefs are a mix of Hinduism, Eastern mysticism, pantheism, and many other religions. God offers eternal life, health, and peace only through faith in Jesus Christ as God and our Savior from sin.

Objectives

The participants, through the study of God's Word and the power of the Holy Spirit, will

1. identify some of the many non-Christian sources of New Age beliefs;
2. affirm the Bible's clear plan for salvation and reconciliation for all people;
3. give thanks for their Spirit-given faith and be willing to share it with others.

If your group responds to creative, hands-on activity, bring in some recent fashion magazines for men and women. Have the participants work in pairs or small groups to find recycled fashions from earlier generations. (You can find lots of fashion information these days through the Internet. Some sites available as this study was written were www.geocities.com/Hot Springs/5164/contrib.html and www.best.com/~lana jean/lecture.html.)

A Look at the New Age

Ask the class how many are familiar with the New Age Movement. Allow one or two volunteers to share what they know about it. Then distribute copies of Resource Page 11A. Call on volunteers to read the various sections. Stop briefly at the end of each section for comments and questions. Emphasize the following points:

History: The New Age Movement does not reject any religion or philosophy. Whatever *seems* right to you *is* right for you.

Central Teaching: New Age followers do not love or depend on God. They *become* god by loving and depending on themselves.

Other Major Teachings: The New Age uses concepts that are familiar to Christians, but gives them different meanings. The Bible teaches, for example, that those who love and trust in Jesus are "born again" (John 3:7), not reincarnated. God says that we die only once (Hebrew 9:27) and awaken when Christ returns (1 Thessalonians 4:16).

Contemporary Encounters: New Age influence is rarely obvious. For example, material intended to build self-esteem is frequently loaded with New Age principles, philosophy, and buzz words. Christians can be influenced by these beliefs without even realizing it.

Christian Connection: The next activity will emphasize the difference between being *like* God and *being* God.

Studying the Word

Sound Good?

You may wish to assign each statement to an individual, pair or small group of students. After a few minutes to study the statement, invite volunteers to share their responses and discuss.

Distribute copies of Resource Page 11B. Read the opening paragraph and examine the three statements. First consider why each statement sounds good and then reconsider it in the light of God's Word. Incorporate these thoughts into discussion:

Statement 1: The statement makes it sound as if our "true spiritual nature" is a real asset. But God's Word shows that, as sinners, our spiritual nature is ugly and perverse. The only way to spiritual freedom is through confession and repentance. It is only in the forgiveness and redemption Jesus has won for us that we find freedom from fear and guilt and confidence in God.

Statement 2: Imagine what a mess we could make of our lives and the lives of others if we made our own rules and were held accountable to no one. When we follow our own desires, our hearts become hardened to God's love, and we do not listen to His voice. In God's Word we have an absolute standard of truth.

Statement 3: Unity sounds good and God-pleasing. But spiritual unity can only come through faith in Jesus Christ as a person of our Triune God. Jesus said, "No one comes to the Father except through Me" (John 14:6).

Ask the participants to turn to 1 John 3:1–2, read the passage to themselves, and respond to the question. The passage says we are greatly

74

loved children of God, people who will be like Him, people who will get to see Him when He returns. Point out that the passage says we will be "like Him," not that we will *become* Him. Reiterate that we can be confident about God's love and care for us.

Applying the Word

What Now?

Read the opening line in this section. Then invite a volunteer to locate and read aloud 1 John 2:20–25 and verse 28. Say, "Do you hear what God is saying to us? We have it made! He is addressing us as friends, as insiders, people who know what's going on!" Point out how this passage prepares and encourages us for encounters with New Age thinking?

- It reminds us of the Holy Spirit at work in us (anointing—verse 20).
- It reminds us that we have the truth of God's Word to guide us (verse 21).
- It shows us a handy way of identifying New Age or any other kind of un-Christian thinking (verses 22–23).
- It reminds us that the truth about Jesus has been around since the beginning and has stood the test of time (verse 24).
- It reminds us of God's promise to us (verse 25).
- And it commends and motivates us (verse 28).

As narrow-minded and uncompromising as it may seem, to respect Jesus merely as a good man, a prophet, or an "ascended master" denies the power of His death and resurrection to give us "new life." Remind students of Jesus' exclusive claim in John 14:6 and that staying on the narrow path (Matthew 7:13–14) requires us to be *narrow*-minded!

Direct the participants to the word picture at the resource page. Point out the two radically different kinds of worship depicted and ask, "How is it that we 'choose' one over the other?" (The way we live is a result of the faith in our hearts and the new life we have through Christ. We live "in Him" by God's grace and by His power.) Point out that the diagram shows the tools and practices we use for each kind of worship. Name each one and let a volunteer tell briefly what it is. Use the following definitions to clarify the terms.

Chants: Songs or recitations repeated over and over to encourage inward focus for meditation.

Crystals: Natural rock or stone formations that are believed to have healing or energizing powers.

Mind-altering drugs: LSD, marijuana, and other chemicals are used to produce altered states of consciousness that increase spiritual awareness.

Faith in self: We are our own best source of provision, healing, and restoration.

Hypnosis: A psychically induced state that leaves the mind open to external manipulation.

Ouija board: A tool for communicating with the spirit world.

Psychics: People who claim to have cosmic power, energy, or insight.

Resources

How to Respond: The New Age Movement, Philip H. Lochhaas, CPH, 1995

The New Age Is Lying to You, Eldon K. Winker, CPH, 1994

Relativity: The absence of absolute standards or values where choices always depend on variables.

Spirit guide: A nonphysical personality who communicates through a medium or *channel.*

Tarot cards: A deck of 78 cards that supposedly can reveal the secrets of the universe.

Bible study: Not just reading, but studying God's Word to understand and apply it.

Holy Communion: Receiving the body and blood of Jesus Christ for forgiveness and spiritual strength.

Faith in God: Looking to God as the ultimate source for provision, healing, and restoration.

Fellowship: A supportive relationship among the people of God as brothers and sisters in Christ.

New Life: Living according to the will of God through the power of the Holy Spirit at work in us through God's Word so that we reflect His love.

Praise: Words and acts that celebrate the greatness of God.

Prayer: Mental or verbal conversation with God; talking and listening to Him.

Repentance: A change of mind and heart motivated by the Holy Spirit from wrongdoing to obedience.

Thanksgiving: A statement, act, or attitude of appreciation for God's love and provision.

Truth: Reality according to God.

Closing Prayer

Conclude by reminding the participants that the New Age Movement is not new. Ever since the Garden of Eden, Satan has been tempting us to be our own god. Invite the class to join in a circle prayer asking God for forgiveness for the times we let Satan trick us into being our own god, for protection from Satan's evil schemes, and for wisdom to better recognize God's truth.

Start the prayer yourself: "Heavenly Father, thank You so much for Your mercy. We are so eager to do things our way, and we're always messing up. Please forgive us." Allow time for participants to offer their prayers aloud and silently. When all have had an opportunity to pray, conclude: "Lord we ask these things in the name of our Lord and Savior—Your Son, Jesus Christ. Amen."

New Age Thinking—Everyone and Everything Is God?

History

The New Age Movement is a postmodern blend of many old religious concepts. It has no specific leader, no special headquarters and claims no sacred writing as its own. The New Age Movement does not even consistently identify itself as a religion. It might best be described as a loose network of organizations and individuals who believe that humankind can and must "fix" themselves and the world through enlightened thinking. Its beliefs come mainly from various Eastern religions (Hinduism, Buddhism, and others), the occult (magic, astrology, tarot cards, and various other practices), and distortions of Christianity.

Central Teaching

Despite the many differences in various New Age practices and beliefs, most New Age followers advocate personal and social transformation through self-development, cosmic evolution, spiritism, and political action. According to New Age thinking, the reason for social problems and disharmony is our failure to realize our unlimited personal potential.

Significant People

The New Age Movement adopts the deities, founders, and prophets of several other religions as spiritual role models. Jesus, for example, is one of many "ascended masters"—people who recognized their divine capabilities and used them. Other significant figures of the New Age Movement are celebrities, such as actress Shirley MacLaine, television producer Norman Lear, and the late singer-actor John Denver, who have openly embraced the movement, giving it credibility.

Other Major Teachings

Everything is God; God is not a person but an impersonal consciousness or force found in everything. The New Age Movement seeks to help people discover "the God within" through various spiritual exercises and therapies. Christ is not a person but a position, a level of "divine consciousness" that anyone can attain. The movement encourages toleration, rejects absolutes, and embraces all forms of spiritual striving including reincarnation, *karma* (actions in this life determine our status in the new), *channeling* (communicating with gods, spirits, and the souls of the dead through mediums), psychic healing, and enlightened "Christ-consciousness."

Contemporary Encounters

The New Age influence is subtle but pervasive. Its influence can be seen in modern self-help movements (TM, yoga, and Zen), in school curricula (secular humanism), in popular music styles (New Age music), and in the themes of many movies and television programs (including some by producers George Lucas, Steven Spielberg, and Gene Rodenberry).

Christian Connection

We are made in the image of God, but we are not God! God is our loving Father—not "a force." God offers eternal life, health, and peace only through faith in Jesus Christ as God and our Savior from sin.

 One God, Many Gods

Sound Good?

The New Age Movement invites our interest and support with noble and righteous-sounding appeals. Why do these statements sound so good? How are they contrary to the Word of God?

Honest acceptance of one's true spiritual nature leads to freedom from all grief, fear, bitterness, guilt, and the endless need that plagues human life.

(Romans 3:10-18, 23-24)

We limit and enslave ourselves when we allow others to tell us the truth instead of discovering it and even creating it for ourselves. The spiritual *person determines what is right and true one moment at a time.*

(Ephesians 4:17-24)

We have a unique opportunity at this time in history to focus on the profound and meaningful messages of the world's religions and to bring about a new "unity of spirit."

(Romans 15:5-7)

Our only defense against the subtle deception of New Age thinking is faithful confidence in who we are in Christ. Who does God say that we are in 1 John 3:1-2?

What Now?

God calls us to new and eternal life in Jesus Christ. Read God's words of encouragement in 1 John 2:20-25, 28. **Through our faith, God empowers us to live according to His will for us.**

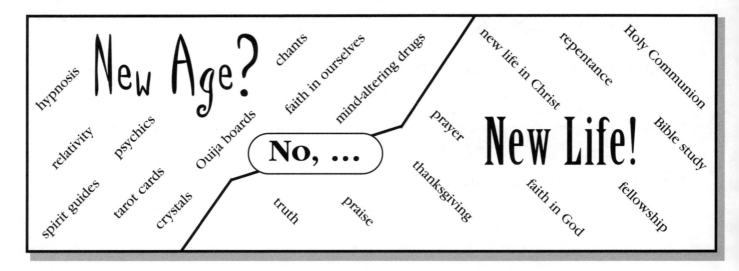

One God, Many Gods   **Resource Page 11B**

Atheists, Agnostics, and Skeptics

Questions about the Existence of God

John 9; Hebrews 11:1

Study Outline: Atheists, Agnostics, and Skeptics

Activity	Time Suggested	Materials Needed
Opening Activities (Choose one)		
An Improbable Possibility	10 minutes	
A Response to Doubt	10 minutes	Copies of Resource Page 12A
Studying the Word		
Responding in Faith	20 minutes	Bibles
Applying the Word		
The Hope We Have	15 minutes	Copies of Resource Page 12B; Bibles
Closing Prayer	5 minutes	

Opening Activities

An Improbable Possibility

Engage the participants in a simple quiz on statistical probability. For each question below read the three possible responses and challenge the participants to guess the correct one.

1. What is the possibility of being hit by lightning during your lifetime?

   a. 1 in a million

   b. 1 in 9,000

   c. 1 in 1,000

   (The correct answer is b.)

2. The probability of dying in a plane crash?

   a. 1 in 400,000

   b. 1 in 800,000

   c. 1 in 2 million

   (The correct answer is a.)

3. The possibility of being hit by a meteor?

   a. 1 in a million

   b. 1 in a billion

   c. 1 in 5 billion

   (The correct answer is c.)

4. The possibility of injuring yourself so badly while shaving that it would require medical attention?

    a. 1 in 7,000

    b. 1 in 12,000

    c. 1 in 100,000

    (The correct answer is a.)

5. The probability that you will die?

    a. 1 in 1,000

    b. 1 in 100

    c. 1 in 1

    (The correct answer is c.)

6. The possibility that you would get bitten by a poisonous creature in your lifetime?

    a. 1 in a million

    b. 1 in 21 million

    c. 1 in 35 million

    (The correct answer is b.)

7. The possibility that all we see, including ourselves, is a random act of evolution and chance?

    a. 1 in a million

    b. 1 in a billion

    c. 1 in 1,000,000,000,000,000,000,000 ("10 to the 20th power")

    (The correct answer is c, according to the former atheist and evolutionary scientist Sir Fred Hoyle.)

Remind the class that many things in life can be expressed in terms of statistical probability. Throughout history, many people have concluded that God's existence is probable, based on such things as the grandeur of the universe, the consistency of the cosmic order, and the complexity of the human body. They wager, to use Blaise Paschal's phrase, that God *does* exist and that it is completely reasonable to believe in a Creator and Lord of all things. For Christians, God's existence is not just probable, but certain. "Now faith is being sure of what we hope for and certain of what we do not see" (Hebrews 11:1). Share that this study will help us answer, lovingly and reasonably, those who deny or doubt God's existence.

A Response to Doubt

Distribute copies of Resource Page 12A. Briefly review the six sections of the page. Stress these simple definitions:

- Atheists believe there is no God or supreme being.
- Agnostics struggle with concepts associated with God, religion, Christianity, and the like.
- Skeptics are unsure if there is a God and believe that no one can really know.

Then ask of each viewpoint, "Why might people believe this way?" List volunteered responses on newsprint or on the board, accepting all suggestions.

The resource page describes one of the main reasons that people reject God. It is said that either God isn't all-loving or He isn't all-powerful—He either doesn't love us or care about the suffering in the world, or He is powerless to stop it. Life is full of such difficult questions.

Studying the Word
Responding in Faith

Lead the group through this three-step Bible study process.

Step 1

In groups of three or four, invite the participants to give some examples of bad things that have happened to them or to people they know. Limit this sharing time to about five minutes. Encourage volunteers to be brief and not to reveal confidential information.

Step 2

Read John 9, the entire chapter. You can have each person read it silently, or ask volunteers to read it aloud. Then discuss these questions:

1. **What was wrong with the man?** (The man had been blind since birth.)

2. **What were some assumptions that people had about his blindness?** (People assumed that the man was blind because of his sins or the sins of his parents.)

3. **Knowing what you know about evil, was it fair for this man to be blind?** (We can debate what is fair and what isn't. His blindness, and all physical infirmity and human frailty, results from the introduction of evil into the world when Adam and Even fell into sin.)

4. **Why did the Pharisees object to Jesus healing the man's blindness?** (See verse 16 and verses 28–29.) (The Pharisees accused Jesus of doing work on the Sabbath. They accused the once-blind man of being one of Jesus' disciples, part of a growing movement that they did not believe was God's work but that of the devil.)

5. **What did Jesus share with the man that really gave him sight?** (See verse 39. Jesus shared that He was the true Messiah, who came to bring eternal life.)

6. **What didn't the Pharisees "see"?** (See verses 40–41. The Pharisees refused to admit their sin and need of a savior. They believed their good deeds would save them from God's wrath.)

7. **How did God use this evil—the man's blindness—for good?** (God used the man's blindness to heal him spiritually—to show

An Optional Activity

Collect the front page of each day's newspaper from the past week. Distribute them to the class and invite the participants to search for bad things that have happened to people. Use these recent, real-life examples to introduce this topic or to demonstrate the reality of evil in our world and why bad things might happen to sometimes seemingly good people.

Christ's redeeming love to him and to many others. This man will now see for all eternity!)

Point out that adversity does not contradict faith. God can, and frequently does, use adversity to bring people to faith, or to strengthen the faith that is already theirs.

Step 3

Share the following story with the class:

In the November, 1997, issue of The Lutheran Witness *a touching story is told of a missionary, Merrell Wetzstein, and his serious illness. In October 1996, he was diagnosed with brain cancer and all medical attempts to bring it under control failed. He died early in 1998. However, God used Merrell's illness to His glory and the spreading of God's Word. Merrell ministered to people suffering the same illness and continuously pointed to the work of the cross and the certainty of his salvation. The faith that God gave him in spite of this terrible disease has led others to Christ.*

Invite the participants to share their reactions to the story, how God has used those bad things in their lives to bring hope, joy, and comfort in others, and how that has strengthened their faith. If your group is large, do this in the small groups from step 1. Allow about five minutes for this sharing.

Wrap this section up by pointing to the Good News that God, through the cross, has given us new life through Christ in this life and eternal life with Him in heaven. Through the Holy Spirit He gives us confidence in His presence and power and helps us reflect His love to others.

Applying the Word
The Hope We Have

Distribute copies of Resource Page 12B. Have participants look up 1 Peter 3:15. Then discuss the questions on the page, incorporating these suggested responses:

1. The verses encourage us to be prepared to give an answer concerning the hope we have in life.

2. Our manner of response should be loving and patient.

3. Through our faith in Jesus Christ, we have the certain hope—forgiveness for sin and eternal life with God.

Discuss with the class what would they do in the situations on the resource page. If your class is large, or if you are short of time, assign each situation to a small group or pair of participants. Affirm those who find ways to address the situations with testimonies of faith and assurances of God's love.

It may be helpful to write these prayer-starters on newsprint or on the board so that participants can refer to them during the prayers.

Closing Prayer

Say, "We can be thankful that God created us and loved us enough to die for us. In a world of doubt, we can have confidence in Him. That's the hope we have. We all have friends, family, or those we know that really don't understand or know that God loves them. Let's take time to pray for them." Encourage the participants to complete these two prayers silently; then conclude the prayer as indicated.

- "Lord God, I'm thankful You created me because _____." (Pause for silent prayer.)

- "Lord, help me reach the person who doesn't know you by _____." (Pause for silent prayer.)

"Heavenly Father, You loved us so much that You sent Your Son to die for us. Help us reflect Your love to others so that they too can have faith in You. In Jesus' name we pray. Amen."

For Further Study

People live in a world of pain, hurt, and confusion. If their home isn't effected by drug and alcohol abuse, divorce, or other serious problems, they certainly have friends whose homes are. The questions of evil and why it happens—where is God, if there really is a God—are very real issues for many. Our ability to listen, care, and show compassion can assist such people. A solid, biblical understanding of the issue of evil and the precious message of the Gospel are even more important as tools used by the Holy Spirit to bring them faith and new life.

Check out these Bible passages and the truth they share with us: Romans 8:31–39, 2 Corinthians 5:16–21, 2 Corinthians 12:7–10, and Job 1–3 and 40–42.

Resources

False Gods of Our Time, Norman Geisler, Harvest House, 1985

Handbook of Today's Religions, Josh McDowell and Don Stewart, Campus Crusade for Christ, Inc., 1983

Atheists, Agnostics, and Skeptics—Questions about the Existence of God

History

Questions about the existence of God are as old as humankind and the development of these schools of thought tends to overlap considerably. Skepticism is the oldest, emerging in the fourth century B.C. in Greek schools of philosophy, fading as Christianity grew, and surfacing again after the Reformation in Western Europe. Contemporary agnosticism was advanced in the eighteenth and nineteenth centuries. The roots of atheism can be seen in the sixteenth-century A.D. writings of Machiavelli and others, but modern atheism was developed in the nineteenth and twentieth centuries.

Central Teaching

The atheist believes that there is no god, the skeptic doubts that possibility and struggles with issues surrounding God, the agnostic claims that no one can know. All three insist that there are no rational or intellectual grounds to believe in God.

Significant People

Skepticism: Contemporary proponents include A. J. Ayers (1920–1970) and Albert Camus (1913–1960).

Atheism: Georg Hegel (1770–1831), Karl Marx (1818–1883), Friedrich Nietzsche (1844–1900), Jean-Paul Sartre (1905–1981), and others. Madalyn Murray O'Hair has gained prominence in America through her organization, American Atheism.

Agnosticism: David Hume (1711–1804), Immanuel Kant (1724–1804), and T. H. Huxley (1825–1895).

Other Major Teachings

- It is meaningless to talk about God, because He is not empirically verified (that is, by observation).
- We can't know realities such as God, but only our perceptions of reality.
- God as Christians describe Him cannot exist, because a loving God could not allow evil. God defies logic and therefore cannot be real.
- God is a result of wishful thinking or superstition.

Contemporary Encounters

Though they share some common ground, these three philosophies are very different from each other in many ways, including their visibility. Atheism, and skepticism to a lesser degree, tend to be more aggressive and organized movements. Many of their advocates create campus organizations and advertise their view through Internet websites.

Christian Connection

The religious atheists, agnostics, and skeptics of this world all miss an important truth. "Now faith is being sure of what we hope for and certain of what we do not see" (Hebrews 11:1). Our certainty about God and the salvation He has provided for us in His Son comes *through faith*, which is God's gracious gift as the Holy Spirit works through the Word.

Scripture quotation: NIV®. Used by persmission of Zondervan.

The Hope We Have

Step 1

Look up 1 Peter 3:15, then discuss;

1. What simple advice does this verse give us?
2. What are some ways we can do that?
3. What is the hope that we have? (Remember John 9.)

Step 2

In the following situations how might you respond in faith?

1. Your friend just shared with you that she has been diagnosed with leukemia? She continually asks, "Why me?" *What do you share? How do you respond?*

2. You are out having pizza with a group of your friends. Someone states, "What's the big deal about religion? Aren't they all the same thing anyway? Who is to say which one is right or wrong?" *What do you say? How do you respond?*

3. You become friends with someone at work. As you get better acquainted, you discover that your new friend isn't really sure that there is a God. Your friend states that the important thing isn't what you say you believe, but how people treat each other. *What do you say? How do you respond?*

4. You attend a science lecture, and the speaker states that it is foolish that people still believe that God created the world considering all the proof we have about evolution. *What do you say? How do you respond?*

 One God, Many Gods

Christianity and Other Religions—A Comparison Chart

Christianity

History

The Christian church dates its beginning from Pentecost in A.D. 30. The church was essentially one body for a thousand years. A split between the East and West in 1054, the Reformation movement in the sixteenth century, and other divisions in the past 500 years have resulted in hundreds of denominations today.

Central Teaching

Christians recognize Jesus to be the Christ (the *Anointed One* or *Messiah*) sent by God to redeem all people from sin. Jesus is both God and man (Colossians 2:9, Isaiah 9:6, 2 John 7). Any religion that does not acknowledge Jesus as Lord and Savior is not Christian (1 John 4:1-6).

Significant People

- Jesus' disciples—12 chosen men, including Peter, James, and John, and many others.
- Paul, who converted to Christianity about five years after Jesus' resurrection and brought Christianity to people throughout the Roman empire.
- Augustine of Hippo (354–430) provided leadership during a series of major controversies.
- Martin Luther (1483–1546), who preached that we are justified by grace alone, through faith in Christ alone, as taught by Scripture alone.

Judaism

History

Judaism traces its roots back to Abraham in 2,000 B.C. God's promises to Abraham (Genesis 12:1-3) and His covenant (Genesis 15:1-21) begin the relationship between God and the Jews.

Central Teaching

God is a personal, all-powerful, eternal, and compassionate God. His history with His people and His basic teachings are found in the *Torah*, the first five books of the Old Testament. Judaism also accepts as true the entire Old Testament and the *Talmud*, a 2,700-page record of the teachings of ancient rabbis.

Significant People

In addition to Abraham, the other Old Testament patriarchs are considered giants of the faith. King David also is revered because under him Israel became a mighty world power.

Judaism stresses obedience to the Law (the Ten Commandments). While they acknowledge the necessity of God's mercy since no one can perfectly keep the Law, they do not acknowledge the substitutionary sacrifice of Jesus. Atonement for sin is made through works of righteousness, prayer, and repentance. Many Jews believe in a physical resurrection. Judaism does not accept Jesus Christ as the promised Messiah.

There are around six million Jews living in the United States. Almost every major city has at least one Jewish synagog.

Most Jews will be familiar with Jesus, but they won't acknowledge Him as the Savior. Because of their belief that the Messiah has not yet come, we can witness to Jews by celebrating the hope we have in Jesus. An active, dynamic faith that openly confesses Jesus is the best witness.

Other Major Teachings

The Christian church is united by many common beliefs in the one message of salvation through Christ, including the Trinity; the Bible as God's Word; sin is universal to human beings; the Law and Gospel; eternal life as God's gift; and the sacraments as tools God gives the church to work faith, forgiveness, and the assurance of eternal life.

Contemporary Encounters

Nearly a third of the world's population describes themselves as Christian. Though there are hundreds of denominations, the church is united in belief in the triune God, the Bible as God's Word, and salvation through Jesus.

Christian Connection

Central to the Christian faith is the belief that Jesus, God's only Son, is both fully human and fully divine. He suffered and died so that we might receive God's gift of forgiveness of sins. He fulfilled all the Law so that we might receive God's gift of Christ's righteousness.

One God, Many Gods, © 1998 CPH

Buddhism

History

Buddhism arose in India about 500 B.C. Siddartha Gautama found that his Hindu beliefs did not adequately explain the suffering and pain he observed in the world. Through religious contemplation, Gautama became *Buddha*, "the enlightened one," and taught others his discoveries.

Central Teaching

Pure Buddhism is more philosophy than religion, a godless pietism. Other forms of Buddhism revere Buddha as a deity and speak of salvation through faith in him. Buddhism is a journey to an enlightened state of being. People do this by accepting the *Four Noble Truths* and following the *Eightfold Path*.

Significant People

Founder: Siddartha Gautama (Buddha) about 562–480 B.C. Other major teachers: Nichiren A.D. 1222–1282 in Japan and the Dalai Lama, currently living in exile from Tibet in Dharmasala, India.

Hinduism

History

One of the world's oldest religions, Hinduism developed between 1800–1000 B.C. in India. Hinduism contains many sects. Hinduism is both a religion and as a way of life. It is described in the *Vedas* (considered the world's most ancient scriptures, about 1000 B.C.) and the *Bhagavad-Gita*, an 18-chapter poem.

Central Teaching

Hindus believe that all things are part of God, that souls are reincarnated at death, and that our lives are influenced by *karma* (good and bad actions in this life determine one's status in the next). The goal is *moksha*, release from the cycle of reincarnation to become one with God.

Significant People

Hinduism developed over many centuries; there is no single significant founder or leader. The most famous among its followers is Mahatma Gandhi, who led India to freedom from the British Empire in the early twentieth century.

The Four Noble Truths: (1) life is filled with misery and suffering; (2) this misery and suffering is caused by our selfish desires; (3) misery and suffering can be eliminated by getting rid of selfish desires; and (4) these desires are eliminated by following the Eight-fold Path: (1) right views; (2) right thought; (3) right speech; (4) right conduct; (5) right vocation; (6) right effort; (7) right alertness; and (8) right meditation.

Buddhism is gaining popularity especially among media and sports celebrities. The *middle road* and balanced life of Buddhism are a welcome change from celebrity life. Today, followers number over 300 million worldwide, about 500,000 in the U.S.

Salvation is not achieved by right thoughts and right things. It is a gift given to us by a personal God through the sacrifice of His Son. We receive this gift by faith.

Other Major Teachings

(1) *Brahman* is the "Absolute," present in everything. (2) Individuals create their own destinies. (3) Souls evolve through reincarnation. (4) One's place is fixed in a *caste* or level of society. (5) Moksha can be achieved through meditation. (6) A *guru* helps guide a person toward total realization of God. (7) Other important beliefs are personal discipline and observance of many rites and rituals. (8) New Hindus receive names that may change more than once in their lifetime as a result of spiritual events. (9) All life is sacred. (10) No particular religion teaches the only way to salvation above all others.

Contemporary Encounters

The New Age movement and Transcendental Meditation are popular movements founded on Hinduism. Meditation and yoga have become common forms of stress release in our society with classes offered at local colleges and fitness centers.

Christian Connection

According to God's Word, salvation is found only in the saving work of the triune God (Acts 4:12). Although Christians are to live in obedience to God, their salvation is not dependent on this (Ephesians 2:8–9).

Islam

History

In A.D. 610, a businessman named Muhammad (570–632), in Mecca in Saudi Arabia, began to preach submission to the one God *Allah*. He did this as a result of a vision of the angel Gabriel, who gave him the *Qur'an*, Islam's sacred scriptures. Today, Islam is the religion of about 20 percent of the world's population.

Central Teaching

The central confession in Islam is the *shahada*, "There is no God but Allah, and Muhammad is his prophet." *Muslim* means "one who submits." Islam teaches submission to God in all things. It is a code of honor, a system of law, and a way of life based on the Qur'an. The level of devotion to this moral code determines one's salvation.

Significant People

Muhammad, the founder of Islam, is considered Allah's last and greatest prophet. Muslims also believe that Abraham, Moses, and Jesus are great prophets. Jesus is not considered to be God's Son or the Messiah.

Shinto

History

Shinto, the native religion of Japan, is one of the oldest religions in the world, combining ancient religious practices with such influences as Buddhism and Confucianism.

Central Teaching

Shinto is primarily a form of nature worship. Mountains, rivers, heavenly bodies, and other things are worshiped and personified (for example, *Amaterasu* the sun spirit). Rules, rituals, and worship of *kami* (spirit) help to maximize agricultural harvests and bring blessings to social units or territories while preventing destruction and ill fortune.

Significant People

Shinto has no real founder, no written scriptures, no body of religious law, and only a very loosely organized priesthood. Shinto is a nonexclusive religion, that is, people may practice Shinto along with a second or even third religion. Most Japanese practice Shinto and Buddhism.

Muslims live by the Pillars of Islam: (1) Confession of faith—"there is no God but Allah, and Muhammad is his prophet." (2) Daily prayer in the direction of the Sacred Mosque in Mecca, Islam's holiest city. (3) Charity—giving two percent of their annual income to the poor. (4) Fasting at various prescribed times, especially during Ramadan, the holiest month of the Muslim year. (5) Pilgrimage—A pilgrimage to the city of Mecca, the birthplace of Muhammad, is expected of healthy and otherwise qualified Muslims at least once in a lifetime. This event draws well over two million pilgrims each year.

Islam is the world's fastest-growing religion and is visible in North America especially on college campuses and in large communities. A 19th-century heretical off-shoot, *Baha'i*, believes that another prophet, *Baba'u'llah*, was the last and greatest.

The important Christian teaching to keep in mind when encountering Islam is that Jesus is not just a prophet: He is the Son of God, Savior of the world, and God's promised Messiah who died on the cross for the forgiveness of our sins.

Other Major Teachings

Practitioners of Shinto use four *affirmations* ("things we agree are good") to describe their basic beliefs: (1) affirmation of the tradition and the family; (2) affirmation of the love of nature; (3) affirmation of physical cleanliness; and (4) affirmation of *matsuri* (festivals honoring the spirits). Prayers and sacrifices to ancestors can be offered at family altars where ancestors are visibly present in tablets. For important decisions and important occasions of one's life, ancestors are consulted, that is, their graves are visited for reflection and meditation.

Contemporary Encounters

In North America there is a large and growing number of Japanese immigrants. They have imported their gardens with tori gates and other animistic features. Many of them will continue to hold Shinto beliefs even as they "try out" other religions.

Christian Connection

We have a powerful message to share with those of Shinto faith—Jesus Christ has paid everything we owe, performed all the duties that are required, suffered, died, and rose from death so that we can be free from sin and have new life in Him.

Mormonism

History

The Church of Jesus Christ of Latter-day Saints was begun by Joseph Smith, Jr., in 1830, in Fayette, New York. Smith claims to have translated the *Book of Mormon* from golden "tablets" entrusted to him by the angel Moroni. In 1844, Smith and his brother were imprisoned and killed. Brigham Young moved the group to the Salt Lake valley where it flourished.

Central Teaching

Mormons believe that God was once a human being just like us and that we can become gods and earn admittance to a celestial heaven.

Significant People

In addition to Joseph Smith, Jr. (1805–1844), and Brigham Young, other important early leaders included Oliver Cowdery, who figured prominently in the founding, and Sidney Rigdon, an early convert and theologian in the Latter-day Saints who was passed over for leadership at Smith's death.

Satanism

History

The term satanism is applied to many cults and movements, some of which pre-date the time of Christ and among which there is little unity. Even today, different satanic organizations vary in beliefs and practices.

Central Teaching

Traditional satanism emphasizes worship of a powerful, personal devil through cultic ritual and black magic. This form has not disappeared. Modern satanists frequently reject worship of Satan, but advocate instead that everyone indulge in whatever activity they want, without limit or restraint. This often includes satanic practices.

Significant People

- Aleister Crowley (1875–1947) was an early leader of modern satanism in Great Britain. Raised in a Christian home, he became devoted to magic and the occult. Crowley started his own satanic group.
- Anton Szandor LaVey (1930–1997) was the force behind modern satanism. In 1966 LaVey formed the Church of Satan. He wrote *The Satanic Bible* and *The Satanic Rituals*. Since his death, LaVey's daughter Karla has assumed leadership of the Church of Satan.

Mormons do not believe in a triune God, but in three gods who are "united in love and purpose." There are three heavens; to reach the highest one, you must believe that Smith and his successors are true prophets, be baptized a Mormon, live a good life, obtain a celestial marriage, bear many children, attend all church functions, pay tithes to the church, and avoid alcohol, hot beverages, and tobacco. Mormon doctrine includes progressive revelation—the most recent revelations of the current living prophet supersede previous doctrines.

Tabernacles have been erected in all parts of the United States and are under construction or planned for all major continents. Mormon membership has grown to more than 8.3 million members worldwide, 4.5 million in the United States.

Christians bear witness to the one triune God through whom we have salvation by God's grace alone, not by our efforts. The Bible is God's unchanging truth and our only authority for teaching.

Other Major Teachings

The Church of Satan follows these guidelines for behavior: (1) Prayer distracts people from useful activity. (2) Enjoy indulgence instead of abstinence. (3) If someone smites you on one cheek, smash him on the other. (4) Do unto others as they do unto you. (5) Engage in sexual activity freely in accordance with your needs. (6) Suicide is frowned upon. (7) The satanist needs no detailed list of rules of behavior. (*Adapted from a satanism website.*) Satanism appeals to sinful instincts and supports Satan's ends by telling sinners exactly what they want to hear.

Contemporary Encounters

Satanism is a do-it-yourself religion that can spring up anywhere. It is usually stumbled into by unsuspecting people who are open to its lies because they seek excitement, easy solutions to their problems, or power over others through magic.

Christian Connection

The truth of God's Word is a powerful weapon against Satan. Christians can share the truth of Jesus Christ with Satan's followers, confident that he has ultimately been crushed through Christ's suffering, death, and resurrection.

Scientology

History

Scientology was founded in 1954 by L. Ron Hubbard. The movement began with the popularity of Hubbard's book, *Dianetics: The Modern Science of Mental Health.*

Central Teaching

Using the methods of Scientology, people are capable of raising their own spiritual awareness to the point of achieving immortality. Those who reach this level are called *operating thetans* (thay-tns).

Significant People

Scientology is based solely on the many writings of L. Ron Hubbard. Among the members of the Church of Scientology are numerous celebrities, including John Travolta, Tom Cruise, Kirstie Alley, and Lisa Marie Presley.

Jehovah's Witnesses

History

Charles T. Russell (1852–1916) founded *The Watchtower Bible and Tract Society* in Pennsylvania in 1872. The group become officially known as Jehovah's Witnesses in 1931. The Witnesses claim world-wide membership of over 5.5 million with over 20 percent of them in the United States.

Central Teaching

Jehovah's Witnesses believe that they have been organized to announce the early establishment of God's rule on earth.

Significant People

Charles T. Russell was the founder and author of most of the *Studies in the Scriptures* that outline the group's teachings. His successor, Joseph F. Rutherford, moved the organization to Brooklyn, New York, and established the governing body, a small group of men who continue to direct the work and determine the teachings of the Witnesses.

Students of Scientology, called *preclears*, are first taught a method called *auditing* that is designed to clear their mind of *engrams* (negative mental images). Once students reach a state of *clear*, they follow the steps on the *bridge to total freedom* with the goal of becoming operating thetans.

Operating thetans are said to have "complete spiritual freedom," including immortality.

L. Ron Hubbard's writings are widely available in bookstores. *Dianetics*, his most famous title, is widely marketed as a self-help book. Scientology benefits from endorsements, donations, and public appearance from its celebrity members.

Thanks be to God that, as Christians, we do not have to rely on ourselves for salvation! In our Baptism, we are claimed by a God "who has saved us and called us to a holy life—not because of anything we have done but because of His own purpose and grace" (2 Timothy 1:9).

Scripture quotation: NIV® Used by permission of Zondervan.

Other Major Teachings

The Witnesses use *The Watchtower* to interpret the Bible and as their main means for spreading their doctrine. They also have their own version of the Bible called the *New World Translation*. They believe that Jesus Christ, who is the "created" son of God but not God Himself, was sent to earth to be a perfect and blameless human to pay for Adam's sin. This opens the door for us to prove our worthiness. The Witnesses deny hell and claim that only 144,000 will be in heaven while the rest of the faithful will be on the new earth.

Contemporary Encounters

It seems likely that most everyone will encounter Jehovah's Witnesses at their own doorstep at some time or another. Door-to-door witnessing is the only activity of members on which records are kept and the most important requirement for their salvation.

Christian Connection

Christians share three important truths with the Witnesses: (1) the Bible is the only source for all our knowledge about God and His plan for salvation; (2) salvation is not earned by good works, but is ours by God's grace through faith in Jesus Christ; and (3) Jesus Christ is true God, and all who believe in Him have forgiveness for sin and eternal life.

Atheists, Agnostics, and Skeptics

Skepticism emerged in the fourth century B.C. in Greek schools of philosophy. Agnosticism was advanced in the eighteenth and nineteenth centuries. The roots of atheism can be seen in the sixteenth century, but modern atheism was developed in the nineteenth and twentieth centuries.

The atheist believes that there is no god, the skeptic doubts that possibility and struggles with issues surrounding God, the agnostic claims that no one can know. All three insist that there are no rational or intellectual grounds to believe in God.

Skepticism: Contemporary proponents include A. J. Ayers (1920–1970) and Albert Camus (1913–1960).
Atheism: Georg Hegel (1770–1831), Karl Marx (1818–1883), Friedrich Nietzsche (1844–1900), Jean-Paul Sartre (1905–1981), and others. Madalyn Murray O'Hair has gained prominence in America through her organization, American Atheism.
Agnosticism: David Hume (1711–1804), Immanuel Kant (1724–1804), and T. H. Huxley (1825–1895).

New Age Thinking

History

The modern New Age Movement is a postmodern blend of many old religious concepts. It is a loose network of organizations and individuals who believe that humankind can and must "fix" themselves and the world through enlightened thinking, including beliefs from various Eastern religions, the occult, and distortions of Christianity.

Central Teaching

Most New Age followers advocate personal and social transformation through self-development, cosmic evolution, spiritism, and political action. According to New Age thinking, the reason for social problems and disharmony is our failure to realize our unlimited personal potential.

Significant People

The New Age Movement adopts the deities, founders, and prophets of other religions as spiritual role models. Jesus, for example, is one of many *ascended masters*—people who recognized their divine capabilities and used them. Other significant figures of the New Age Movement are celebrities, such as actress Shirley MacLaine, television producer Norman Lear and the late singer-actor John Denver, who have openly embraced the movement, giving it credibility.